INVESTIGATOR'S GUIDE TO STEGANOGRAPHY

OTHER AUERBACH PUBLICATIONS

The ABCs of IP Addressing
Gilbert Held
ISBN: 0-8493-1144-6

The ABCs of LDAP
Reinhard Voglmaier
ISBN: 0-8493-1346-5

The ABCs of TCP/IP
Gilbert Held
ISBN: 0-8493-1463-1

Building an Information Security Awareness Program
Mark B. Desman
ISBN: 0-8493-0116-5

Building a Wireless Office
Gilbert Held
ISBN: 0-8493-1271-X

The Complete Book of Middleware
Judith Myerson
ISBN: 0-8493-1272-8

Computer Telephony Integration, 2nd Edition
William A. Yarberry, Jr.
ISBN: 0-8493-1438-0

Electronic Bill Presentment and Payment
Kornel Terplan
ISBN: 0-8493-1452-6

Information Security Architecture
Jan Killmeyer Tudor
ISBN: 0-8493-9988-2

Information Security Management Handbook, 4th Edition, Volume 1
Harold F. Tipton and Micki Krause, Editors
ISBN: 0-8493-9829-0

Information Security Management Handbook, 4th Edition, Volume 2
Harold F. Tipton and Micki Krause, Editors
ISBN: 0-8493-0800-3

Information Security Management Handbook, 4th Edition, Volume 3
Harold F. Tipton and Micki Krause, Editors
ISBN: 0-8493-1127-6

Information Security Management Handbook, 4th Edition, Volume 4
Harold F. Tipton and Micki Krause, Editors
ISBN: 0-8493-1518-2

Information Security Policies, Procedures, and Standards: Guidelines for Effective Information Security Management
Thomas R. Peltier
ISBN: 0-8493-1137-3

Information Security Risk Analysis
Thomas R. Peltier
ISBN: 0-8493-0880-1

Interpreting the CMMI: A Process Improvement Approach
Margaret Kulpa and Kurt Johnson
ISBN: 0-8493-1654-5

IS Management Handbook, 8th Edition
Carol V. Brown and Heikki Topi
ISBN: 0-8493-1595-6

Managing a Network Vulnerability Assessment
Thomas R. Peltier and Justin Peltier
ISBN: 0-8493-1270-1

A Practical Guide to Security Engineering and Information Assurance
Debra Herrmann
ISBN: 0-8493-1163-2

The Privacy Papers: Managing Technology and Consumers, Employee, and Legislative Action
Rebecca Herold
ISBN: 0-8493-1248-5

Securing and Controlling Cisco Routers
Peter T. Davis
ISBN: 0-8493-1290-6

Six Sigma Software Development
Christine B. Tayntor
ISBN: 0-8493-1193-4

Software Engineering Measurement
John Munson
ISBN: 0-8493-1502-6

A Technical Guide to IPSec Virtual Private Networks
James S. Tiller
ISBN: 0-8493-0876-3

Telecommunications Cost Management
Brian DiMarsico, Thomas Phelps IV, and William A. Yarberry, Jr.
ISBN: 0-8493-1101-2

AUERBACH PUBLICATIONS

www.auerbach-publications.com
To Order Call: 1-800-272-7737 • Fax: 1-800-374-3401
E-mail: orders@crcpress.com

INVESTIGATOR'S GUIDE TO STEGANOGRAPHY

Gregory Kipper

AUERBACH PUBLICATIONS

A CRC Press Company

Boca Raton   London   New York   Washington, D.C.

Library of Congress Cataloging-in-Publication Data

Kipper, Gregory.
   Investigator's guide to steganography / Gregory Kipper.
      p. cm.
   Includes index.
   ISBN 0-8493-2433-5 (alk. paper)
      1. Computer security. 2. Cryptography. 3. Data protection. I. Title

QA76.9.A25K544 2003
005.8'2--dc22

2003056276

Visit the Auerbach Publications Web site at www.auerbach-publications.com

© 2004 by CRC Press LLC
Auerbach is an imprint of CRC Press LLC

No claim to original U.S. Government works
International Standard Book Number 0-8493-2433-5
Library of Congress Card Number 2003056276
Printed in the United States of America 1 2 3 4 5 6 7 8 9 0
Printed on acid-free paper

Dedication

For my family and friends

Dedication

Contents

About the Author

Greg Kipper, CISSP, works as an IT security consultant and computer forensics investigator in the Washington, D.C. area.

Acknowledgments

I'd like to thank all the people who encouraged and supported me during this lengthy endeavor. They include my parents and family, Bruce Middleton, Cynthia Hetherington, Pete and Virginia Garfall, Rich O'Hanley, Christian Kirkpatrick, the Auerbach and CRC Press crew, Luke McKinney, Dave and Lisa Stafford, John Stockman, Al Vance, and all the authors and researchers whom I've referenced and learned from. Without you, none of this would have been possible.

Greg Kipper
August 2003

Chapter 1

Introduction

Skewing the Rules

In everyday terms, we expect language to be understandable, reliable, and shared. However, dialects, foreign languages, or communication systems out of our reach or ability can sometimes make understanding difficult. In particular, technology, an agreed-upon code or device/system, is set in place to deliberately hide the true intention of that communication. So what we see is not necessarily what we get. There may be a secret message hidden inside the innocuous message you have before you. In other words, someone has skewed the perspective of what you are reading, hearing, or experiencing to deceive your perception of what is actually being transmitted. Hence, an e-mailed photo of two friends at the park may actually hide a covert message sent from one spy to another.

Whether for fun, profit, or military means, we have been skewing the language rules for centuries. As Kipper's book will demonstrate, mathematicians, military warriors, and scientists have been altering the common language or the means by which we transfer our message to deliberately hide secret communications.

Hiding information in plain sight by altering the image we see, the arrangement of the message, or the language in which it is delivered has become a multi-million dollar industry known as steganography. Threats from abroad, as well as domestic uses for steganography, have kept decoders on their toes.

A Low-Tech, Everyday Example between Two Friends

Two young ladies, Michele and Linda, are in a bar, both looking for "Mr. Right." Michele is patiently waiting in line for the ladies' room when she overhears two men talking to each other. They are looking at Linda, who is still sitting at the bar. "Hey ... I think I'll put the moves on her, she looks pretty fun, and I'll bet easy enough to dump afterwards." Then the man begins to approach Linda; meanwhile, Michele gets her friend's attention. Linda notices that Michele is pushing her hair back with her fingers forming the letter "L" and indicating the man approaching Linda with her eyes. He does not have a chance now. Linda knows from Michele's openly signed but undisclosed message that this guy is a LOSER. To anyone else, Michele was just moving the hair out of her eyes.

Another fun example is Darmok and Jelad at Tenagra.

In a season-five episode of *Star Trek, The Next Generation,* called "Darmok," the Enterprise encounters an alien Tamarian ship at the planet El-Adrel IV, and communication between the alien Captain, Dathon, and our hero, Picard, is attempted by video/radio. The Tamarians cannot be understood, although they use English phrases, including names and events from their culture and mythology. Captain Picard and his first officer discuss the meaning of the Tamarian's phrase, *Darmok and Jelad at Tenagra.* Picard and Dathon transport to El-Adrel IV's surface, where they attempt to communicate.

Things turn ugly and a battle ensues between the two captains; at the same time Picard is trying to understand the language of the Tamarians. Finally, as the two captains struggle to communicate in order to fight effectively, Picard hypothesizes that the Tamarians communicate by example, and the proper names and places they cite are references to situations in their history. Picard is then able to begin to communicate with Dathon, and the alien responds enthusiastically to his efforts.

Picard concludes that the Tamarian language is based on metaphors from Tamarian history and mythology. *Darmok and Jelad at Tenagra* refers to two Tamarian heroes who met on an island, joined together to defeat a terrible monster, and left together. El-Adrel IV is the home of a powerful and monstrous creature, and the hope is that the Federation and the Tamarian people can become friends by jointly killing the monster on El-Adrel IV.

What began and ended as a diplomatic meeting could have cost fictitious lives if Picard did not decipher the message that was given in plain sight.

Multiply these examples by a few thousand times and you get modern steganography with all of its ciphers and software tools; yet, techno terms aside, steganography is passing the message between two parties, hidden in plain sight.

In the real-world, military, law enforcement, and business forms of steganography are used every day. Real lives rely on transmitting coordinates, drop locations, and important facts needed.

Bad guys use it, too. War chalking, hidden Internet transmissions, spy messages going in and out of the country, and even gang markings spray painted on a wall all are means of communicating information covertly.

What started over 4000 years ago with hieroglyphics has moved into a very technical and complicated science. As with many technical sciences, understanding the basics, getting through the rudimentary fundamentals, and finally comprehending the big picture is often not easy. Fortunately, Kipper entertains as he teaches, and offers many practical examples to explain this detail-oriented science. This work is a readable text that you will keep close. Perhaps Kipper has even hidden some messages within his work. You will have to read, learn, and understand to find that answer.

Cynthia Hetherington, M.L.S., M.S.M.
his@data2know.com

Author's Intent

When I was first approached with the idea for this project, I enjoyed the prospect of it being a worthy challenge while at the same time not quite knowing how it would all turn out. When I spoke with friends and associates about it, their first question was usually, "What's the book about?" My reply, "Steganography," would almost always get the same response. "Stega-what?" After going through this a few times, I changed my response from one word to a summarized explanation. My new canned answer became "The book is about a form of hidden communication called steganography."

This explanation was better received, and I began to notice that people who had no interest in computers or criminal investigations were raising their eyebrows at this topic that they had never heard of before. Either that or my brief explanation gave them a connection to something they have seen or heard about in their everyday lives.

It was these observations that got me thinking not just about steganography, but the context of steganography. These thoughts led to the foundations of this book. I set out purposefully and began working through the book's structure, gathering my research materials and observing what I had originally suspected. There was a fair amount of information on steganography, but the information was usually very specific and technical, rarely touching on how it fit into a larger picture.

It is my hope that this book will show the myriad places that steganography has existed in the past and can exist in modern times.

Who Should Read This Book?

The short answer to that question is anyone who is interested in learning more about steganography. But in truth the book is geared more toward the law enforcement and cyber-forensics investigator community. As a forensics investigator, I know that steganography is something other investigators are aware of, but that their knowledge levels can vary dramatically depending on the types of cases they have been exposed to. This book is meant to level the playing field from an "awareness" standpoint. Often, in an investigation it is not necessary to be an expert on one particular topic; what is important is first to be aware of its existence and then to know some of the creative ways it can be used. I do not expect that you will read this book from cover to cover, but you may read a few chapters in a row and use others for reference.

I have structured the book in a way that takes you from knowing nothing to knowing what steganography is and how it fits into the world we live in. The first part of this book covers the basic types of steganography (and there are quite a few), and also some of the events and people that have used steganography throughout history. The second part moves into the specifics of how digital steganography and watermarking work. I took great care in making these sections only as technical as necessary. The goal is to give you a general understanding, not to teach you to write your own steganography algorithm. The third part moves into some of the tools you as an investigator or casual user may encounter on the Internet. This is not a complete list, of course, but it does contain information about a lot of what is out there. The last chapters of the book cover how steganography and watermarking are used in the world and how to detect and defeat them.

I hope you find this book interesting as well as a little entertaining. I hope that it gives you a foundation on which to explore on your own and look in directions you might not have looked otherwise.

Chapter 2

A Basic Understanding

What Is Steganography?

Steganography is a type of hidden communication that literally means "covered writing." The message is out in the open, often for all to see, but goes undetected because the very existence of the message is secret. Another popular description for steganography is "hidden in plain sight." In contrast, cryptography is where the message is scrambled, unreadable, and the existence of a message is often known.

Oftentimes throughout history encrypted messages have been intercepted but have not been decoded. While this protects the information hidden in the cipher, the interception of the message can be just as damaging because it tells an opponent or enemy that someone is communicating with someone else. Steganography takes the opposite approach and attempts to hide all evidence that communication is taking place. We will look at an example of this in the next section.

Differences between Steganography and Cryptography

- *Steganography:* Hides a message within another message and looks like a normal graphic, video, or sound file. *Cryptography:* The message is encrypted; looks like a meaningless jumble of characters.

- *Steganography:* A collection of graphic images, video files, or sound files on a disk may not look suspicious. *Cryptography:* A collection of random characters on a disk may look suspicious.
- *Steganography:* A smart eavesdropper can detect something suspicious from a sudden change of message format (i.e., text to graphic images). *Cryptography:* A smart eavesdropper can detect a secret communication from a message that has been cryptographically encoded.
- *Steganography:* Requires caution when reusing pictures or sound files. *Cryptography:* Requires caution when reusing keys.
- *Steganography:* There are no laws associated with steganography. *Cryptography:* There are some laws that ban cryptography.

Differences between Steganography and Watermarking

Watermarking and steganography differ in an important way: Steganographic information must never be apparent to a viewer unaware of its presence; this feature is optional when it comes to watermarking.

Modern steganography should be detectable only if secret information is known, namely, a secret key.

The Prisoners' Problem

Simmons describes an excellent, common example of steganography in what is called the "Prisoners' Problem." Alice and Bob are the two fictional characters in this example, and they have been arrested and placed in different cells. Their goal is to develop an escape plan and bust out of jail; the snag is that the only way to communicate is through the warden, Wendy. Being a capable warden, Wendy will not allow Alice and Bob to communicate in code (encryption), and if she should notice anything suspicious, one or both of them will immediately be put in solitary confinement. So Alice and Bob must communicate in a manner that does not arouse suspicion; they must communicate invisibly using steganography.

The example goes on to explain that a smart way of doing this is to hide the information in an innocuous-looking message or picture. Bob could draw a picture of a blue cow in a green pasture, and ask Wendy to pass it along to Alice. Wendy would, of course, look at it before passing the picture and, thinking it is just a piece of abstract art, would pass it along, not knowing that the colors in the picture conveyed the message.

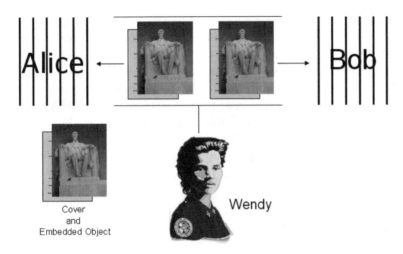

Figure 2.1

While this can work on paper, there are some problems that could stop the escape. Wendy may alter the picture, either accidentally or purposely, and therefore alter the message. If Wendy purposely altered the picture, thereby destroying the message, it would be considered an active attack. Going further with this idea, we will assume that Wendy creates a forged message of her own and passes it to one of the prisoners while pretending to be the other. This is considered a malicious attack.

The Prisoners' Problem model can be applied to a lot of situations where steganography can be used for communication. Alice and Bob are the two parties who want to communicate and Wendy is the eavesdropper, and while this model can be an effective means of communication, the potential of passive, active, or malicious attacks must always be considered.

Figure 2.1 shows the components that make up the basic framework of what it takes to communicate using steganography. Take a look at each piece individually: cover object, stego-key, and stego-object. The cover object is what is actually going to be seen out in the open, the picture, sound, or movie that will be used to carry the message right under everyone's noses. The stego-key is the code that the person sending the secret message is going to use to embed the message into the cover object; this same stego-key will be used by the recipient to extract the secret message. Stego-keys can come in many forms; they can be a password or an agreed-upon place to look for the hidden message. The stego-object is the combination of the cover object, the stego-key, and the secret message. These three combine to create the condition where a cover object is carrying a secret message.

Now that we have looked at the basics of steganography and how it is used to communicate, we will go into some real-world techniques that have been used in the past to illustrate some of the inventive forms that steganography can take and the effectiveness it can have. These methods and techniques that I will be describing are nondigital and are meant to act as a primer for the next section on history. Again, as I stated in the introduction, this book is meant to educate you not only on what steganography is, but also on how it fits into the world. These techniques are not listed in any particular order, and are meant to lay the foundation for the next section.

Microdots

The microdot is a page-sized photograph that has been reduced to 1 mm in diameter. The microdot became a popular and commonly used form of steganography during World War II. The process of creating a microdot is straightforward, but requires a few specialized pieces of equipment. First, a photograph of the message is taken, and this reduces it to roughly the size of a postage stamp. Next, the image is shrunk further with a reverse microscope, bringing it down to 1 millimeter. The negative is then developed and the image is punched out of the film. A common way to do this was with a syringe needle in which the point had been filed down. Once the needle separated the dot from the rest of the film, it was placed on the cover text, over a period or under a stamp, and cemented in place.

Professor Walter Zapp is credited with creating a device that could perform most of these processes mechanically.

One-Time Pads

A one-time pad is a method of encoding a message with a random key once and only once. This type of encoding is an unbreakable system because no matter how much time or sample text a cryptanalyst has available, breaking the code would be impossible. The cipher would never be the same twice.

Semagrams

A semagram is nothing more than a symbol. Its literal meaning is, in fact, semantic symbol. Semagrams are associated with a concept and do not use writing to hide a message. Do you remember our example in the Prisoners' Problem? Bob sent a picture to Alice; the picture or, more specifically, characteristics about the picture conveyed the secret information. A semagram can be almost anything that does not use words to hide a message. You will see more on semagrams when I cover World War II in the next section.

Null Ciphers

A null cipher is an unencrypted message crafted in such a way that the real message is "camouflaged" in a larger, innocent-sounding message. A null cipher is also sometimes referred to as an open code. Null ciphers have one big drawback: They do not always "sound" quite right. The message may read clumsily, and suspected messages can be detected by mail filters. Although innocent sounding, messages often go undetected and are allowed to flow through.

Following are some examples of messages containing null ciphers:

> News Eight Weather: Tonight increasing snow. Unexpected precipitation smothers eastern towns. Be extremely cautious and use snowtires especially heading east. The highways are knowingly slippery. Highway evacuation is suspected. Police report emergency situations in downtown ending near Tuesday.

By taking the first letter in each word, the following message can be derived: *Newt is upset because he thinks he is President.*

> Fishing freshwater bends and saltwater coasts rewards anyone feeling stressed. Resourceful anglers usually find masterful leapers fun and admit swordfish rank and overwhelming any day.

Taking the third letter in every word, the following message emerges: *Send lawyers guns and money.*

Anamorphosis

Anamorphosis is a technique in which an image, or the production of an image, appears distorted unless it is viewed from a special angle or with a special instrument. This is a rather obscure form of steganography, but it has been used in the past and deserves mention. The word anamorphosis is Greek and means "change shape." It is meant

Figure 2.2

to imply a transformation the viewer effects by shifting his or her perspective (Figure 2.2).

Acrostics

Acrostics are one of the most benign forms of cipher. Much like a null cipher, an acrostic is blended into a poem or series of lines in which certain letters, usually the first in each line, form a name, motto, or message when read in a particular sequence. Acrostics were very popular with poets during the Italian Renaissance and they can also be found frequently in Elizabethan literature.

Type Spacing and Offsetting

Type spacing or type offsetting is a way of subtly distorting the text in a message to hide additional data. Type spacing was created as a way to discourage illegal copying of textual material. While this makes its intended purpose as a form of watermark, type spacing can also be used to send a message in secret. To encode a secret message using type spacing all one would have to do is adjust specific letters ever so slightly from their normal position. The letters that are out of position indicate the secret message.

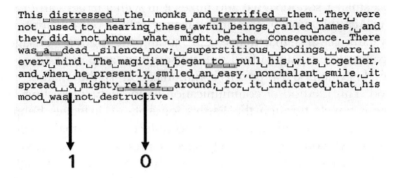

Figure 2.3

This form of steganography can be used with a good deal of flexibility by either adjusting the white space between the letters or the words, or by slightly shifting entire blocks of words from their original position. This is the nondigital form of this type of steganography (Figure 2.3).

The digital approach uses the actual positions of the lines or the words in the document to indicate a 1 or 0 position. These subtle position shifts are created and detected by the stego-algorithm, which when run will indicate a 1 or 0 and, ultimately, the hidden message.

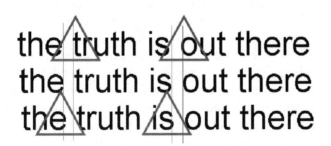

Figure 2.4

Spread Spectrum

Spread-spectrum steganography is the method of hiding a small or narrow-band signal (message) in a large or wide-band cover. This technology has been developed and used since the 1950s to provide a method of communication that is hard to intercept or jam. Similar to hiding a message within a picture, spread-spectrum steganography takes a smaller sound signal and mixes it in with a larger carrier signal. This makes this type of transmission very robust because there is so much extra cover signal that is surrounding the hidden message that it becomes like trying to find one person in a large crowd.

Another method of covert communication is the meteor scatter method. This method of communication is uniquely interesting. When a meteor travels through the Earth's ionosphere, it leaves behind an ionized trail. This trail can be used to reflect radio signals over great distances. As you might expect, special procedures are used when using the meteor scatter method. Typically, prearranged schedules are made outlining the time, frequency, and sequencing of the messages. Because the majority of the meteors falling allow a signal to be reflected for only a very short time, roughly a fraction of a second, a method called HSMS (High Speed Meteor Scatter) is often used. This method has been popular in Europe for many years and is now gaining popularity in North America.

Invisible Ink

Invisible inks are colorless liquids that require heat, light, or a special chemical to change their colors and make them visible. The basics behind reactions that do not use heat involve an acid or a base and a pH indicator. The colorless liquid, which is either an acid or base, is applied to paper and dried, making it invisible. When a pH indicator is introduced, it reacts with the acid or base properties of the dried liquid and changes color. There have been several types of liquids used throughout history that work well as invisible inks: milk, vinegar, lemon juice, and even urine. Often, invisible inks were not as easy as milk and lemon juice; they sometimes required complex procedures to prevent enemy censors from discovering them.

Following are some examples of invisible inks that have been used by spies in the past:

■ Cobalt oxide dissolved in hydrochloric or nitric acid produces a liquid that is invisible until it is held up to a flame, at which point it glows blue. The blue will then disappear by blowing on the sheet.
■ Eggs have been used to hide secret messages. A message is written on the shell of a clean egg and the ink diffuses through the porous surface of the shell. When the egg is boiled thoroughly, the shell is carefully peeled off, revealing the message.

Newspaper Code

During the Victorian era, newspapers could be sent without charge; the poorer classes of the time made use of this and invented the newspaper code. The process could not be more straightforward. Holes were poked just above the letters in the newspaper so that when the dots were transferred and written together the secret message would be revealed. While this method of steganography took a fair amount of time, it did allow people to communicate freely.

Newspaper codes resurfaced during World War II and into the Cold War, although during this time the pinholes were replaced by either secret ink markings or invisible ink, which made the codes much harder to detect. Unfortunately, the newspaper code in the twentieth century had one big drawback: speed. Newspapers were sent as third-class mail, which often took quite a while for a message to be sent. Usually, war conditions had changed by that time. In addition, the man-hours required by American censors quickly made checking every newspaper clipping impractical, and eventually all newspapers were banned from entering the country.

Jargon Code

A jargon-coded message changes words instead of replacing individual letters. Jargon code is word-crafting at its finest and usually requires a good bit of imagination on the part of the sender. A good number of years ago I worked summers at Disneyland as one of the boat drivers on the Jungle Cruise. After being there for a couple of weeks I was introduced to the local jargon code, which the male employees used when an attractive woman was within eyeshot. The word was "Alp" and it was surprisingly effective for those of us who knew what to listen for. This one word allowed a few guys to effectively communicate in crowds of several hundred people at a time without drawing undue attention. I realize this example could be the simplest form of jargon code; normally, it is more than just one word, but it illustrates the point of communicating out in the open quite well without anyone noticing.

Grilles (Cardano's Grille)

Named for its inventor, Girolamo Cardano (1501–1576), the Grille system works in the following way: Each recipient has a piece of paper or cardboard with holes cut in it (the grille). When the grille is placed over an innocent-looking message, the holes line up with specific letters in the message, revealing the hidden message within.

Intercepting these messages becomes very difficult at this point because the larger message, which often takes up a page, completely blends the shorter, secret message into it. As with jargon code, this type of steganography requires imagination and good writing skills. Cardano's Grille is considered one of the safest ways to transmit a secret message.

Bibliography

Bailer, W., *wbStego,* available at http://www.8ung.at/wbailer/wbstego/sg_li000.htm, 1998.

Friedman, W.F. and Friedman, E., *The Shakespearean Ciphers Examined,* Syndics of the Cambridge University, U.K., 1958.

Kahn, D., *The Codebreakers,* Macmillan, New York, 1967.

Katzenbeisser, S. and Petitcolas, F.A.P., *Information Hiding: Techniques for Steganography and Watermarking,* Artech House, Boston, 2000.

Kent, P., Art of Anamorphosis, available at http://www.anamorphosis.com/.

Low, S.H., Maxemchuck, N.F., Brassil, J.T., and O'Gorman, L., *Document Marking and Identification Using Both Line and Word Shifting,* AT&T Bell Laboratories, New Jersey, 1994.

Schilling, D.L., *Meteor Burst Communications: Theory and Practice,* Wiley Europe, 1993.

Simmons, G.J., "The Prisoners' Problem and the Subliminal Channel," CRYPTO83, *Advances in Cryptology,* August 22–24, 51–67, 1984.

Zim, H.S., *Codes and Secret Writing,* William Morrow, New York, 1948.

Chapter 3

History

While doing my research for this chapter, I came to realize that the further I dug, the more interested I became. I think you will find this loosely chronological layout very interesting. I wanted to include an in-depth section on history for many reasons, mainly as a logical starting point, a basis to gain some perspective about steganography and its uses. But, most importantly, this chapter will show you and, ultimately, educate you about some of the extremely inventive ways that steganography has been used in the past. While the bulk of this book deals with digital forms of steganography, there are no rules that say an opponent or attacker cannot revert back to an old, analog method. So this chapter's main goal is to make you aware of some things you may not have thought of on your own.

This chapter also makes mention of a few people throughout history who have made a contribution to cryptography rather than steganography. I have included them because these people often did some work that influenced the work of someone later, someone who did use steganography.

The Egyptians

The Egyptians, through their use of hieroglyphics, are considered the first to use cryptography. Hieroglyphic writing uses characters in the form of pictures. A hieroglyph can be read as a picture or a symbol for a picture or a sound. In a town called Menet Khufu some 4000 years ago, a scribe used hieroglyphics to tell the story of his master's life. While hieroglyphics are not thought of as a form of secret writing in the modern world, some hieroglyphics were stylized in such a way that only those who knew what to look for could read them properly. This meager distinction can be considered one of the first instances of steganography.

The Greeks

The Greeks get credit for using steganography in a few inventive ways. Herodotus, who documented the conflict between Persia and Greece in the fifth century B.C., felt that the art of secret writing saved Greece from Xerxes, the tyrant king of Persia. The trouble, and the use of steganography, began after Xerxes began building his new capital at the city of Persepolis. Gifts began arriving from all over the empire with the exceptions of Sparta and Athens. This insult to Xerxes brought the long-running feud between Greece and Persia to a head. Deciding to teach the Greeks a lesson, Xerxes spent the next five years amassing the largest fighting force in history, and in 480 B.C. he was ready to launch his surprise attack.

Fortunately for the Greeks, the Persian military buildup had been witnessed by Demaratus. Demaratus was a banished Greek who happened to live in the Persian city of Susa. Demaratus, who still felt a loyalty to Greece in spite of his expulsion, decided to warn the Spartans of Xerxes' plans to invade Greece. Naturally, the difficulty was getting the message to the Spartans without it being intercepted by the Persians. Herodotus wrote:

> As the danger of discovery was great, there was only one way in which he could contrive to get the message through: This was by scraping the wax off a pair of wooden folding tablets, writing on the wood underneath what Xerxes intended to do, and then covering the message over with wax again. In this way the tablets, being apparently blank, would cause no trouble with the guards along the road. When the message reached its destination, no one was able to guess the secret, until, as I understand, Cleomenes' daughter Gorgo, who was the wife of Leonides, divined and told the others that if they scraped the wax off, they would find something written on the wood underneath. This was done; the message was revealed and read, and afterwards passed on to the other Greeks.

This warning to the defenseless Greeks gave them time to arm themselves. The profits of a silver mine, which was owned by the state, were distributed to the citizens; these profits were now given to the navy for the construction of 200 warships. With the element of surprise lost, the Persian fleet sailed into the Bay of Salamis near Athens to face a very prepared Greek navy. The Greeks, knowing that their warships were smaller, fewer, and would not last long on the open sea, lured the Persian fleet into the harbor where they had the advantage of maneuverability in a confined space. The Persians, realizing this, attempted a retreat but were blown into the bay by a change of winds. At this point the Greeks launched a full attack and did significant damage to the Persian fleet in less than a day.

In "The Histories," Herodotus documented another instance where steganography was used. A Greek named Histaiaeus wanted to encourage Aristagoras of Miletus to revolt against the Persian king, and did so in a rather inventive way. In order to pass these instructions securely, Histaiaeus shaved the head of his messenger, wrote the message on his bare scalp, and then waited for the hair to grow back. While this certainly is not the quickest method of communication, it was very effective because the messenger was able to pass guard inspections without harassment because he was carrying nothing suspicious. When the messenger reached his destination and the intended recipient, his head was shaved and the message read. Similar to this was the instance where a rabbit's belly was shaved, the message written, and the hair allowed to grow back, making the rabbit the stego-medium rather than the person.

Another, more subtle mention of steganography was found in Homer's *Iliad*. As the story goes, Bellerophon was being enticed by Anteia, who happened to be the King's wife. When Bellerophon refused her advances, Anteia cried rape. The King ordered Bellerophon to go to Lycia and to carry an enciphered message with him to their King. The message to the King happened to contain Bellerophon's execution order. On reading the enciphered message, the King decided not to execute him and instead married him off to his own daughter.

Æneas the Tactician

Æneas the Tactician is one of the more-famous Greeks, thanks in large part to his book, *On the Defense of Fortified Places,* which was the first instruction manual of its time for communications security. Æneas developed a steganography system whereby holes representing letters of the Greek alphabet were bored into a wooden disk. Yarn was then threaded through the holes in an order that would spell out the message. The decoder would simply reverse the process, writing the letters down backwards, to reconstruct the message.

Another method Æneas suggested was pinning tiny holes above or below specific letters in a document, thus spelling out the message. This steganographic system, called the newspaper code, was still used into the twentieth century.

The Chinese

The Chinese used a slightly different form of steganography. Like the Greeks, the Chinese would transport secret information via messengers. The object was called a La wan, a thin piece of silk that had a message written on it. The silk was then rolled into a ball of wax, which was carried by a messenger somewhere on his or her person.

There is another example in history of the Chinese using steganography during the Yuan dynasty when China was ruled by the Mongolian Empire. The leaders from the preceding Sung dynasty were unhappy living under foreign rule and set out to coordinate a rebellion without it being discovered. The leaders of the rebellion decided to use the upcoming Moon Festival to coordinate their attack. The Moon Festival has a special tradition, the eating of moon cakes. The rebels had messages baked into each moon cake that outlined their attack plans. On the night of the festival, the cakes and the attack plans were distributed, and the rebels successfully attacked and overthrew the government. What followed was the Ming dynasty. Moon cakes are still eaten today in memory of this event.

Gaspar Schott

Gaspar Schott, in his book *Schola Steganographica,* described a method of encoding secret information by matching letters to specific musical notes. This "music" would never be pleasing to listen to if played, and to the untrained eye it would appear to be normal sheets of music when, in fact, it was an encoded message (Figure 3.1).

Johannes Trithemius

The monk Johannes Trithemius, considered one of the founders of modern cryptography, had ingenuity in spades. His three-volume work,

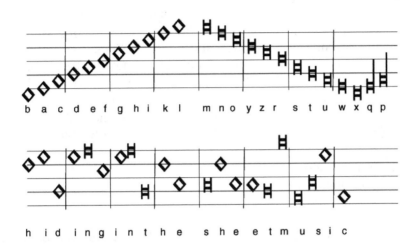

b a c d e f g h i k l m n o y z r s t u w x q p

h i d i n g i n t h e s h e e t m u s i c

Figure 3.1

Steganographia, written around 1500, describes an extensive system for concealing secret messages within innocuous texts. On its surface, the book seems to be a magical text, and the initial reaction in the sixteenth century was so strong that *Steganographia* was circulated only privately until publication in 1606. But less than five years ago, Jim Reeds of AT&T Labs deciphered mysterious codes in the third volume, showing that Trithemius' work is more a treatise on cryptology than demonology. Reeds' fascinating account of the code-breaking process is quite readable.

One of Trithemius' schemes was to conceal messages in long invocations of the names of angels, with the secret message appearing as a pattern of letters within the words, for example, as every other letter in every other word:

```
padiel aporsy mesarpon omeuas peludyn malpreaxo
```

which reveals "prymus apex."

Another clever invention in *Steganographia* was the "Ave Maria" cipher. The book contains a series of tables, each of which has a list of words, one per letter. To code a message, the message letters are replaced by the corresponding words. If the tables are used in order, one table per letter, then the coded message will appear to be an innocent prayer.

The modern version of Trithemius' scheme is the Spam Mimic program.

Giovanni Porta

Italian scientist Giovanni Porta was born in 1535 and made contributions both to steganography and cryptography. Porta described how to conceal a message within a hard-boiled egg by making an ink from a mixture of one ounce of alum and a pint of vinegar, and then using it to write on the shell. The solution would penetrate the porous shell, and leave a message on the surface of the hardened egg albumen, which can be read only when the shell is removed.

In his book, *De Furtivis Literam Notis,* he earned himself a place in cryptography's history. Porta classified cryptography into three types:

1. Transposition
2. Substitution by symbol
3. Substitution by another letter

Again Porta's contribution to polyalphabiticity was not particularly great, but he was the first to really bring it out into the open. His contribution helped with the development of cryptography by those who came after him.

Girolamo Cardano

Girolamo Cardano (Figure 3.2) did far more in his life than make a contribution to steganography. Cardano was a skilled physician, an astrologer, and an accomplished mathematician. Cardano wrote 131 books plus manuscripts on a wide variety of subjects from mathematics, astronomy, and physics to chess, gambling, poisons, air, water, dreams, urine, teeth, the Plague, wisdom, morals, and music. But it is his contribution to steganography, the Cardano grille, for which he is remembered.

The Cardano grille system may be something with which you are already familiar. The basics are that each recipient has a piece of paper with several holes cut in it. When the "grille" (the piece of paper with holes) is placed over an innocuous-looking message, the holes in the grille line up with words in the larger message to produce the hidden message. Anyone intercepting the message will be nescient to the fact because the words the grille sees have been hidden in a larger message that takes up the entire page. Providing that the sender is a decent wordsmith with a good imagination, even difficult messages can be

Figure 3.2

sent with the grille while the larger message will still be literate and sound meaningful.

The Cardano grille is perhaps the safest way to transmit concealed messages, if performed correctly. Unfortunately, it does not lend itself well to large, concealed messages. An alternative to the Cardano method is the jargon code.

Blaise de Vigenere

Another famous name in cryptography history, Blaise de Vigenere made further advances in the polyalphabetic substitution system. Studying the works of Trithemius, Cardano, and Porta, he was the first to create the auto-key system of cryptography, which was forgotten until it was reinvented in the nineteenth century.

Auguste Kerchoffs

Although his contribution was not to steganography, Auguste Kerchoffs is one of the best-known names in the field of cryptography. His contributions to modern cryptography deserve very honorable mention. Kerchoffs' book, *La Crytographie Militaire,* was one of the more revolutionary of its time. His insights differed from his predecessors in that Kerchoffs looked for new answers to problems that new or changing conditions put on cryptography, and he did so brilliantly.

The most notable new problem of the time was to find a form of cryptography that would work well with a new form of communication: the telegraph. Kerchoffs addressed the issue from the point of view of using military cryptography practices. The principles he put forth are still being used today:

1. The system should be, if not theoretically unbreakable, unbreakable in practice.
2. Compromise of the system should not inconvenience the correspondents.
3. The key should be easily remembered without notes and should be easily changeable.
4. The cryptograms should be transmittable by telegraph.
5. The apparatus or documents should be portable and operable by a single person.
6. The system should be easy, neither requiring knowledge of a long list of rules nor involving mental strain.

Kerchoffs is also credited with a cryptography principle that bears his name, which states that if the method used to encipher data is known by an opponent, then security must lie in the choice of the key.

Bishop John Wilkins

In 1641, Bishop John Wilkins anonymously authored the book *Mercury,* or *The Secret and Swift Messenger* as it was also known. In addition to describing several aspects of cryptography, Wilkins suggested onion juice, alum, ammonia salts, and the "distilled Juice of Glowworms" for glow-in-the-dark writing. Modern invisible inks fluoresce under ultraviolet light and are used as anticounterfeit devices. For example, "VOID" is printed on checks and other official documents in an ink that appears under the strong ultraviolet light used for photocopies.

Mary Queen of Scots

The conspiracy began on religious grounds. Catholic noblemen in England wanted to remove the Protestant queen, Elizabeth, and replace her with Mary, a Catholic. While Mary was not the driving force behind this conspiracy, she would pay the ultimate price for it. Mary had used both cryptography and steganography to communicate with the conspirators by enciphering messages (cryptography) and then hiding them for transport in kegs of beer (steganography).

Unfortunately for Mary, Queen Elizabeth's principal secretary, whose name was Francis Walsingham, was also England's spymaster. Walsingham had accumulated enough evidence to put Mary on trial for treason, under accusation of plotting to assassinate Queen Elizabeth and take the English crown.

While the methods of communication used by Mary and the conspirators were inventive, they were not entirely effective. Walsingham had intercepted several of the messages and had the encryption broken, which led to the deaths of several conspirators and, ultimately, to Mary's.

The Culpers and George Washington

Steganography played a role in the Revolutionary War and helped George Washington on many occasions. A man by the name of Benjamin Tallmage organized a group of spies in New York, squarely in the middle of British forces. The ring consisted of five people and used the code name Samuel Culper.

Robert Townsend, a reporter from an American newspaper, used his press access to interact with British troops through social functions deemed newsworthy without drawing any undue attention. The Culpers used a series of dead drops, some of which were so elaborate that they occasionally worked against them. At one point, one of the Culpers was caught up in an attack and lost his horse, which carried secret documents. The private letter from Washington mentioned the Cuplers by their code name, but concealed their true identities, which only Tallmage knew.

This incident caused Tallmage to adopt some new security precautions, including invisible inks. James Jay, a doctor who was living in England, invented the ink. James also happened to be the brother of John Jay, who would eventually become the first chief justice of the

United States. The invisible ink was used on a blank piece of paper; after the message was written, it was reinserted into a ream of new paper. Washington knew how to find the hidden message by counting from the top down to a specific sheet. He would then apply a second solution to make the ink appear. A concern of Washington's was that carrying around blank sheets of paper would draw suspicion; he ordered that the invisible ink be used on a regular message and the secret message be written between the lines or under the message.

Along with invisible inks, the Culpers used one other method of secret communication. While this method could also be considered cryptography, it is safe to say that it could also fall into the category of steganography and deserves mention.

Washington and the Culpers would use a codebook that had hundreds of common words and would assign a two- or three-digit code to them. Here is a partial sample of the code and translation from George DeWan's paper "Crafty Codes of American Spies":

> 729 29 15th 1779. Sir. Dqpeu Beyocpu agreeable to 28 met 723 not far from 727 & received a 356 ... Every 356 is opened at the entrance of 727 and every 371 is searched, that for the future every 356 must be 691 with the 286 received.

Translated, it reads:

> Setauket August 15th 1779. Sir. Jonas Hawkins [an early messenger] agreeable to appointment met Culper Jr. not far from New York and received a letter ... Every letter is opened at the entrance of New York and every man is searched, that for the future every letter must be written with the ink received.

The Pigeon Post into Paris 1870–1871

During the Franco-Prussian War, which lasted from 1870–1871, Paris was under complete siege and all regular communications were cut off from the rest of France. This complete halting of communications was due to the efficiency of the Prussians, who moved into Paris only six weeks after the war began. As in any wartime situation where communications are disrupted, there is always an attempt to get them back; postmen continued to try to carry messages in and out of Paris, but they were usually captured and sometimes shot. Another attempt by the citizens of Paris was to send sheepdogs out of the city by way of balloons, with the hope that they would carry a message back to the city from the outside. They were never seen again.

By this point the besieged Parisians turned to the only option they had left: carrier pigeons. On the inception of this idea to use carrier pigeons to transport messages, 1000 pigeons were moved into the city. There was, of course, time spent and mistakes made, but on September 27, 1870, the first pigeon flew out of Paris carrying a secret message. On October 1, the pigeon returned.

While this method of communication did turn out to be successful, it was by no means a certainty. Natural predators, hunters, and the general dangers of wartime conditions made this a very dangerous job for the pigeons, and some never returned. But during the course of the war, the carrier pigeons delivered several official dispatches and over 95,000 private messages.

At first the messages were written on thin pieces of paper, tightly rolled, and attached with a piece of thread to one of the tail feathers. Later, a photographer in Paris named Dagron developed a form of microphotography to be used to shrink the written messages even further, and more detailed communiqués were then possible.

By the war's end in 1871, other European powers had taken notice of this form of communication and set up their own "pigeon sections" within their armies. It was only when wireless communications became common that the need for carrier pigeons became obsolete.

Civil War Rugs

A form of steganography was used prior to the Civil War to help slaves escape to freedom. In their book *Hidden in Plain View: A Secret Story of Quilts and the Underground Railroad,* Tobin et al. tell about a code that has been passed down through the generations.

In the 1800s, the Underground Railroad was one of the main escape routes used by slaves. Quilts, which were hung outside to dry, became an ideal way to display information inconspicuously. The quilts would have special patterns sewn into them, which would convey messages to prepare or provide direction to escaping slaves who knew what to look for.

In this excerpt from *Hidden in Plain View,* you will see an example of this quilt coding. A code that has been used and passed down through the years goes like this:

> The monkey wrench turns the wagon wheel toward Canada on the bear paw trail to the crossroads. Once they got to the crossroads they dug a log cabin on the ground. Shoofly told them to dress up, put on cotton and satin bow ties. Go to the cathedral church, get married, and exchange double wedding rings. Flying geese that stay on the drunkard's path and follow the stars.
>
> *Monkey wrench:* This block told the slaves to gather their tools and belongings, and get mentally and physically ready for the journey ahead (Figure 3.3).

Figure 3.3

Wagon wheel: This block was a symbol to begin the journey. Many of the slaves would hide in the bottom of wagons under straw or produce. Some wagons had false bottoms for concealing stow-aways (Figure 3.4).

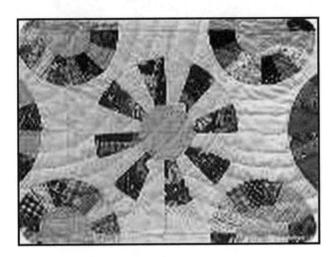

Figure 3.4

Bear paw: This block told slaves to follow bear tracks over the mountain. Bears know the best way to get across a mountain, so following their tracks would lead the slaves safely through the passage (Figure 3.5).

Figure 3.5

Crossroads: This block symbolized the halfway point of the journey (Figure 3.6).

Figure 3.6

Log cabin: This block has a bit of story behind it. It was African tradition that when you passed a stranger you would take a stick and inscribe a symbol of your tribe in the dirt to let the other person know who you were. It acted as a greeting. So to "dig a log cabin on the ground" was a symbol used to communicate with other slaves (Figure 3.7).

Figure 3.7

Bow ties: This block told escaping slaves that it was time for them to shed their old clothes and dress up to better fit into the climate of the city (Figure 3.8).

Figure 3.8

Double wedding rings: This block did not exist until after the Civil War, but the Double Irish Chain quilt did. It symbolized to the slaves the chains that bound them to slavery (Figure 3.9).

Figure 3.9

Flying geese: This block symbolized that it was time to head north. Many slaves, while working or traveling outside, would watch for flocks of geese. They knew when the geese were flying north it was time to follow them (Figure 3.10).

Figure 3.10

Drunkard's path: This block told the slaves not to travel in a straight line because it would be easy for the bounty hunters to find them. Also, in African culture, evil travels in a straight line (Figure 3.11).

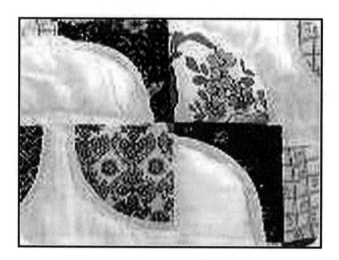

Figure 3.11

Stars: This block symbolized the direction of freedom (Figure 3.12).

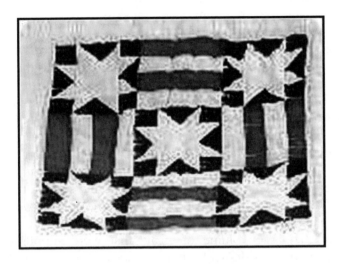

Figure 3.12

World War I

During World War I there were several instances where steganography was used with success. One method was called a Turning Grille, which enhanced Cardano's Grille. It looked like a normal grille, a square sheet of cardboard divided into cells with some of the cells punched out. To use the Turning Grille, the encoder would write the first sequence of letters, then rotate the grille 90 degrees and write the second sequence of letters, and so on, rotating the grille after each sequence.

The Germans provided their troops with different grilles to be used for messages of different lengths and code-named them based on the number of letters in each grille. The French were able to devise an attack against this system, and the grilles lasted only four months.

World War I was also a time in history when cryptography made a giant leap forward. Radio communication, which was used for the first time in a major war, was the biggest contributor to both the need for better cryptography as well as better cryptography security.

Another instance of steganography during World War I was when a woman suspected of working for the Germans was found with a blank piece of paper in the sole of her shoe. As it turned out, this "blank" piece of paper had a message written on it with invisible ink.

The message was quickly revealed because it was written in a heat-based invisible ink. From that point on, the Germans quickly got much more clever and began hiding their messages in garments such as scarves and socks.

Invisible ink subsections were created within the War Department, and a back-and-forth battle began between the Allies and the Germans. At one point in time, 2000 letters a month were being tested, 50 of which had invisible ink messages that proved useful.

There was also a record of a cable censor who received the message "Father is dead." The censor changed the message to "Father is deceased." A reply came back, "Is Father dead or deceased?" Other forms of jargon code were also used during World War I. A British censor was responsible for discovering two German spies when he became suspicious of a large number of cigar orders. The cigar orders were the spies' covert communications, using the numbers and types of cigars to code ship movements. Because of the large volume of cigars that were supposedly being shipped, attention was drawn to their activities. The censor exposed the spies, who were later captured and executed.

World War II

Steganography and its prevention were also prevalent in World War II. After the attack on Pearl Harbor, the United States enacted a censorship organization. This organization worked to think of ways that coded messages could be passed in the open, and took steps to stop them and destroy the code. Chess games were banned by mail; crossword puzzles were examined or removed from correspondence, newspaper clippings, as well as students' grades. At one point, knittings were closely monitored to prevent another Madame Defarge, who passed a number of secret messages during the French Revolution. Stamps were removed and replaced with ones of equal value but different denominations or numbers. Children's pictures were replaced, Xs and Os were removed from love letters, and, of course, blank paper was replaced and tested for invisible ink.

Censor regulations also prohibited sending any text that was unclear, had personal notes not related to the message, or were in a language other than English, French, Spanish, or Portuguese. Censors would often paraphrase messages, and cables ordering flowers forbade any mention of a flower species.

Mass media was also censored. Telephone and telegraph requests for special songs were not allowed, and mail-in song requests would be held for a random amount of time before being played. Personal ads were also censored, including ads for lost dogs. There were no more man-on-the-street interviews, as this could be something an agent could "accidentally" make happen. Children's Christmas lists were also censored.

The *USS Pueblo,* 1968

The *Pueblo* was a U.S. Navy vessel sent on an intelligence mission off the coast of North Korea. On January 23, 1968, the *Pueblo* was attacked by North Korean naval vessels and MiG jets. One man was killed and several were wounded. The 82 surviving crew members were captured and held prisoner for 11 months.

A famous steganographic episode occurred when, in the 1960s, a photograph of several members of the crew of the *Pueblo* was released by their captors in order to demonstrate their cooperation. The seemingly ordinary photograph contained a steganographic message: The hand positions of the crew members spelled the word "snow job" in sign language. In colloquial American English, a snow job means to figuratively cover up or blind someone to prevent them from seeing the truth.

The Vietnam War

Another well-publicized example of steganography happened during the height of the Vietnam War. Commander Jeremiah Denton was a naval pilot who had been shot down and captured. At one point he was taken by the North Vietnamese and paraded around in front of the media as part of a propaganda event. Knowing that he was under the proverbial microscope and unable to say anything openly critical about his captors he blinked his eyes in Morse code, spelling out T-O-R-T-U-R-E, as he spoke to the media.

During the Vietnam era, there were instances where captured members of the U.S. Armed Forces would use various hand gestures during photo ops; often, these gestures were airbrushed out by the media. Prisoners of the infamous Hanoi Hilton used a "tap code" to communicate with each other. The code was based on a five-by-five matrix, with each letter being assigned a tap sequence based on this matrix. Spaces (pauses) between characters were twice as long as the spaces in that letter's code (Table 3.1).

Table 3.1   The 5×5 Tap Code Used by Prisoners in Vietnam

	1	2	3	4	5
1	A . .	B . ..	C, K	D	E . .....
2	F	G	H	I	J .. ..
3	L	M	N	O	P ... .
4	Q	R	S	T	U ....
5	V	W	X	Y	Z ....

U.S./U.S.S.R. Nuclear Arms Treaties

An interesting form of steganography, the subliminal channel, was used between the United States and the U.S.S.R. in 1978. During that time President Carter was heavily involved with the Strategic Arms Limitation Treaty (SALT) talks, which would systematically reduce the number of intercontinental ballistic missiles (ICBMs) between the superpowers. In order to do this to each party's satisfaction, there had to be a protocol in place that allowed the U.S.S.R. to verify the numbers of Minutemen missiles without revealing where the missiles were. This protocol would have to be digitally signed and incapable of being forged. At that time the United States had 100 Minutemen missiles and 1000 silos to hide them in, so it became a shell game of sorts: Keep the Minutemen but keep them safe from a first strike attack by not letting the U.S.S.R. know where they were located.

Margaret Thatcher

Margaret Thatcher, the former British Prime Minister, used a method of invisible watermarking in the 1980s. After several cabinet documents had been leaked to the press, Thatcher ordered that the word processors being used by government employees encode their identity in the word spacing of the document. This allowed for disloyal ministers to be quickly found out.

Bibliography

Carvin, A., *Hidden in Plain Sight: The Debate Over Steganography,* Benton Foundation, 2001, [www.urbanthinktank.org/steganography.cfm.]

Hayhurst, J.D., O.B.E., *The Pigeon Post into Paris 1870–1871,* 1970.

Judge, J.C., *Steganography: Past, Present, and Future*, SANS, 2001.

Kahn, D., *The Codebreakers*, Macmillan, New York, 1967, p. 131.

Maxemchuk, N.F., "Electronic document distribution," AT&T Technical Journal, 73, 5 (Sep/Oct 1994), 73–80.

Pennypacker, M., *George Washington's Spies: In Long Island and New York,* Long Island Historical Society, 1939.

Singh, S., *The Code Book: The Evolution of Secrecy from Mary Queen of Scots to Quantum Cryptography,* Doubleday, New York, 1999.

Spy Letters of the American Revolution: The Culper Gang, June 27, 1779, George Washington to Benjamin Tallmadge.

Tobin, J.L. et al., *Hidden in Plain View: A Secret Story of Quilts and the Underground Railroad,* Anchor, U.K., 2000.

Way, P., *Codes and Ciphers,* Crescent Books, 1977.

Chapter 4

Steganography in Depth

Now that we have covered some of the basic techniques of steganography and how they have been used in the past, we will move forward into the digital age. As I promised in the beginning I am going to keep this as straightforward and nontechnical as possible, but some of these concepts are very technically rooted and will require getting into the weeds, so to speak. I will do my best, but if I get too technical, I apologize in advance.

Steganography Techniques

When it is all said and done, there are only three ways to hide a digital message in a digital cover: injection, substitution, and generation of new files.

Injection

Data injection embeds the secret message directly in the host medium. The problem with this kind of embedding is that it usually makes the host file larger, and therefore the alteration is easier to detect.

Substitution

Normal data is replaced or substituted with the secret data. This usually results in very little size change for the host file. However, depending

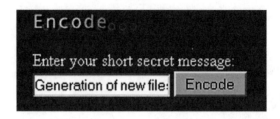

Figure 4.1

on the type of host file and the amount of hidden data, the substitution method can degrade the quality of the original host file.

Generation of New FILES (Figure 4.1)

A cover is generated for the sole purpose of concealing a secret message. As illustrated in "The Prisoners' Problem," Bob creates a picture of something innocent that can be passed to Alice; the innocent picture is the cover that provides the mechanism for conveying the message, which in that example was the particular color of a cow.

Another, more modern form of generation of new files is the Spam Mimic program. Spam Mimic embeds a text message within a rather daunting piece of spam, which can be e-mailed to an intended recipient. While this generated spam does not make a whole lot of sense, it makes enough to be believable, and that is enough.

Resulting Spam Containing the Secret Message

> Dear Friend, Your email address has been submitted to us indicating your interest in our newsletter. We will comply with all removal requests. This mail is being sent in compliance with Senate bill 1623 ; Title 3 ; Section 302. This is NOT unsolicited bulk mail ! Why work for somebody else when you can become rich inside 51 MONTHS. Have you ever noticed how long the line-ups are at bank machines and nobody is getting any younger ! Well, now is your chance to capitalize on this ! WE will help YOU increase customer response by 180% and deliver goods right to the customer's doorstep ! You are guaranteed to succeed because we take all the risk ! But don't believe us. Prof Anderson who resides in Idaho tried us and says "Now I'm rich, Rich, RICH." We assure you that we operate within all applicable laws ! We BESEECH you - act now ! Sign up a friend

and your friend will be rich too ! Thank-you for your serious consideration of our offer ! Dear Professional ; This letter was specially selected to be sent to you ! This is a one time mailing there is no need to request removal if you won't want any more ! This mail is being sent in compliance with Senate bill 1625 ; Title 1 ; Section 304. This is a legitimate business proposal. Why work for somebody else when you can become rich in 49 weeks ! Have you ever noticed nobody is getting any younger and nobody is getting any younger. Well, now is your chance to capitalize on this ! We will help you SELL MORE & use credit cards on your website. You are guaranteed to succeed because we take all the risk. But don't believe us ! Ms Ames of Arizona tried us and says "Now I'm rich many more things are possible." We assure you that we operate within all applicable laws ! We beseech you - act now ! Sign up a friend and you'll get a discount of 20% ! Cheers.

The Six Categories of Steganography

In all methods of steganography, something is done to conceal a message; naturally, these actions or techniques can be separated and analyzed to learn what is happening during the whole process. The six categories of steganography are:

1. Substitution system techniques
2. Transform domain techniques
3. Spread spectrum techniques
4. Statistical method techniques
5. Distortion techniques
6. Cover generation techniques

Substitution System

Substitution system steganography replaces redundant or unneeded bits of a cover with the bits from the secret message. Several steganography tools that are available use the Least-Significant Bit (LSB) method of encoding the secret message. LSB works like this: In a digital cover (picture, audio, or video file), there is a tremendous amount of wasted or redundant space; it is this space that the steganography program will take advantage of and use to hide another message, on the bit level, within the digital cover.

For example, the following string of bytes represents part of a cover, a picture:

```
10000100  10000110  100001001  10001101
01111001  01100101  01001010  00100110
```

Each byte is comprised of eight bits; these bits make up a color value in our picture, a shade of red, or blue, etc. Now, the bits that make up the byte go from left to right in order of importance to the color value they are representing. For example, changing the first bit in our first string from a 1 (10000100) to a 0 (00000100) will drastically change the color, as opposed to changing the last number from a 0 (10000100) to a 1 (10000101). It is that last bit that is considered the least significant, because changing its value has little effect on the information the byte is representing.

Take a look at how a substitution system in steganography can be used to hide a message. Using our string of bytes

```
10000100  10000110  10001001  10001101
01111001  01100101  01001010  00100110
```

we will introduce our hidden message, which is the number of a locker in a bus terminal, locker number 213:

```
213 represented as a binary number is 11010101.
```

Now, using the least-significant bit method, the 213 message will be blended into our cover. We will do this one byte at a time.

> 10000100: The 0 is replaced by a 1, the first bit in our message.
> 10000110: The 0 is replaced by a 1, the second bit in our message.
> 10001001: The 1 is replaced by a 0, the third bit in our message.
> 10001101: The 1 is left alone because it corresponds to the 1 in our message.
> 01111001: The 1 is replaced by a 0, the fifth bit in our message.
> 01100101: The 1 is left alone because it corresponds to the 1 in our message.
> 01001010: The 0 is left alone because it corresponds to the 0 in our message.
> 00100110: The 0 is replaced by a 1, the eighth bit in our message.

Of the eight bytes of information, only five have been altered, and our message has been embedded. Now, while this example deals with only 8 bytes of data, imagine the amount of redundant information in a cover image that is 500 kilobytes or 1 megabyte. Within all those 1s and 0s are a lot of least-significant bits that can be changed with little or no noticeable difference to the cover image.

The LSB technique is commonly used in steganography applications because the algorithm is quick and easy to use; LSB also works well with gray-scale as well as color images.

The LSB technique does have its drawbacks, though. Sometimes, depending on the pixel, adjusting the LSB can dramatically affect the pixel's properties, making it look out of place in the picture, and therefore subject to detection. This problem can limit the amount of substituted bits, and therefore the size of the secret message. Another problem with this method of message hiding is the picture's resistance to changes. If the picture is cropped or rotated, the algorithm will not be able to find which least-significant bits are part of the message and which ones are just supposed to be there.

Transform Domain Techniques

This technique is also very effective and a little trickier to explain. Basically, transform domain techniques hide message data in the "transform space" of a signal. (If you are saying "Huh?" to yourself, hold on, I will explain.) Every day on the Internet, people send pictures back and forth, and most often they use a JPEG format. JPEGs are interesting in that they compress themselves when they close. In order for this to take place, they have to get rid of excess data, excess bits that would otherwise prevent them from compressing. During compression, a JPEG will make an approximation of itself to become smaller; that change, that approximation, is transform space, and that change can be used to hide information.

Spread-Spectrum Techniques

Direct Sequence

In direct sequence spread spectrum, the stream of information to be transmitted is divided into small pieces. Each of the pieces is allocated to a frequency channel of the spectrum. The data signal, at the point of transmission, is combined with a higher data-rate bit sequence that divides the data according to a predetermined spread ratio. Redundant data-rate bit sequence code helps the signal resist interference and enables the original data to be recovered if any of the data bits are damaged during the transmission.

Frequency Hopping

This technique divides a broad slice of the bandwidth spectrum into many possible broadcast frequencies. In general, frequency-hopping devices use less power and are cheaper, but the performance of direct sequence spread-spectrum systems is usually better and more reliable.

Statistical Methods

Statistical methods use what is called a "1-bit" steganographic scheme. This scheme embeds one bit of information only in a digital carrier, and thus creates a statistical change, even if it is only a slight one.

A statistical change in the cover indicates a "1," a cover left unchanged indicates a "0." This system works based on the receiver's ability to distinguish between modified and unmodified covers.

Distortion Techniques

This method of steganography creates a change in a cover object to hide information. The secret message is recovered when the algorithm compares the changed, distorted cover with the original.

Cover Generation Methods

Cover generation methods are probably the most unique of the six types. Typically, a cover object is chosen to hide a message in, but that is not the case here. A cover generation method actually creates a cover for the sole purpose of hiding information. Spam Mimic is an excellent example of a cover generation method.

Types of Steganography

Now that we have looked at the categories of stego, we will discuss the types of stego. There are two basic types, linguistic and technical.

Linguistic Steganography

Linguistic steganography can be described quite simply as any form of steganography that uses language in the cover. A number of forms of linguistic steganography are covered in the next sections, but the two most basic categories are open codes and text semagrams.

A program that takes advantage of linguistic steganography is NICETEXT, which uses the technique of linguistic steganography in a very inventive way. The goal of NICETEXT is to provide a program that can transform ciphertext (encrypted text) into text that looks like natural language while still providing a cover for the original ciphertext. An added benefit of this type of program is that it can be applied to many different languages. The software works by sampling certain aspects of writing by style or by using context-free grammars (CFG).

NICETEXT relies on large code dictionaries consisting of words categorized by type. A style source selects sequences of types independent of the ciphertext. NICETEXT transforms ciphertext into sentences by selecting words with the matching codes for the proper type categories in the dictionary table. The style source defines case sensitivity, punctuation, and white space independent of the input ciphertext. The reverse process simply parses individual words from the generated text and uses codes from the dictionary table to recreate the ciphertext.

Open Codes

In the case of open codes, the openly readable text is mostly well constructed. It can contain certain words or sentences, certain letters can be in certain places in the text, or words can be hidden in vertical or reversed position.

Masking

In a text there could be sentences or words starting with certain letters, which have another meaning. There can also be metaphors, etc., insofar as all kinds of jargons are, in fact, masking.

Null Ciphers

With null ciphers, the hidden text could be reconstructed by taking the first, second, or whichever letter of each word. Hidden messages could also be found vertically, diagonally, or in reverse. To decode, it could also be necessary to rewrite the open text in another form, for example, with a certain number of letters per line.

Cues

The basic definition of a cue is a certain word that appears in the text and transports the message. This type of steganography was often used in wartime situations to broadcast information to spies or resistance troops in other countries. The easiest example is of a nightly radio show where the listener knows in advance to listen for a particular word during a specific portion of the broadcast. If the word is used during the broadcast, certain instructions are to be followed; if the word is not used, different instructions are to be followed. This method of communication is very effective because of its flexibility; the drawbacks are that cues require a good deal of preparation and usually are not capable of conveying large amounts of information.

Music

Although music does not constitute a language, it is written and does convey meaning to those who know how to read it. As was discussed in the previous section, music has been used in a couple of ways to hide information. One method is to match up each note with a letter and thus write out the code (and in the meantime hope no one played the music). Actually this form of communication could also qualify as encryption, but we will leave that alone for now.

The other method is to play the music in such a way that certain notes at certain times would correspond to specific letters and thus spell out the hidden message. This last method can be considered very robust because the cover, the played music, appears to the untrained listener as just a piece of music.

Jargon Code

Probably the most obvious form of linguistic steganography, jargon code creates a verbal or written message as the cover for the secret information. A jargon-coded message is a lot like a substitution cipher in many respects, but instead of replacing individual letters, the words themselves are changed. Remember the example in the previous section where the phrase "Father is dead" was changed to "Father is deceased," and the response was "Is Father dead or deceased?"

Newspaper Code

The newspaper code was invented and used throughout the Victorian era, back in the day when newspapers could be sent almost anywhere without charge. This method was used by the poor who now had a way to send information for free. Small holes were poked over certain letters in the newspaper, which, when connected, spelled out the message. While this practice was time consuming, it often took newspapers weeks to reach certain locations; it did allow people to communicate freely.

Grilles

The grille, or the Cardano grille as it is most often called, is simply a stiff piece of paper or cardboard with holes positioned around it. The secret message is written in the holes, and then the rest of the message is filled in around it. The only way the message is readable is by the recipient who has the correct grille.

Text Semagrams

Text semagrams work with graphical modifications of the text. They concern details that are tiny but nonetheless visible. There are methods that work without text as well, called real semagrams. Some varieties of text semagrams and real semagrams are described next.

Type Spacing and Offsetting

This form of text semagram uses the white space in a document to denote binary values. The white space can be between the individual words, the sentences, or even between the paragraphs. Almost any combination is possible, but to a point, if the text appears to have too much white space it can be subject to scrutiny. While this form of steganography can work effectively, it has a few big drawbacks. First, if the document is digital any modern word processor would be able to show the spacing irregularities or, worse, reformat the document and destroy the hidden information. The second drawback is that this method does not transmit a large amount of information easily, which can limit its practicality (Figure 4.2).

Tiny Spaces

There are not only spaces between words but also tiny spaces between some letters, either to form a binary code out of the frequency of spaces/no spaces or to indicate that the letter following after the space is part of the secret message.

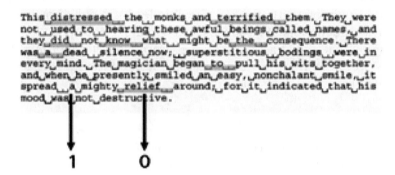

Figure 4.2

Old Typewriter Effect

The old analog typewriter of yesteryear, meaning the Reagan admin-istration, was essentially the same as it was since its creation. It basically operated by a series of gears that allowed the paper to be moved up a specific amount with a carriage return. While this was precise, it was certainly not as precise as today's word processors and laser printers. With some care and attention, deviations could be inserted into a typed document. On some typewriters, making a subscript or superscript setting required a manual rolling of the roller surface to allow a number to be typed, then the wheel would be rolled back to the original position and the typing would continue until the next carriage return. Because this is possible, it goes without saying that making even smaller adjustments while typing is doable and could be used as a way to hide a message, camouflaging it in such a way that it appears that an old or low-quality typewriter was used.

Real Semagrams

A real semagram's practical use is mainly as an indicator of a larger, previously agreed upon message. For example, Bob wants to tell Alice that everything is set for Friday night. A real semagram could be a postcard with a picture of a tropical beach. This could be the agreed-upon code to indicate affirmative. Another semagram with a picture of an Alaskan mountain range could mean negative. A real semagram would not be a practical method of relaying new information. Its best use is to confirm or deny an already agreed-upon course of action.

Technical Steganography

Technical steganography is a little broader in scope because it does not necessarily deal with the written word even though it communicates information. Technical steganography is the method of steganography where a tool, device, or method is used to conceal the message. In reality, linguistic steganography could be considered technical steganography because it is a method. But I am splitting hairs and getting off the subject. We will now take a look at some technical steganography methods.

Invisible Ink

We have pretty much covered all the nuts and bolts of invisible ink. I will not bother to repeat what it is, other than to say it is a special ink that is colorless and invisible until treated by a chemical, heat, or special light. Because invisible ink does not have to be used to write words, it can safely be considered a form of technical steganography. Following are some other examples of invisible ink:

■ Typing a message in typewriter correction ribbon. A message could be written in the white space between the normal black ribbon lines of text and become visible only under a very strong light.
■ Use of hand stamps that are visible only in black light similar to that used in nightclubs and amusement parks.

Hiding Places

This one is a bit obvious so I will not go into great detail on the connections between a hiding place and a way of hiding a message. Hiding places of all varieties fall into the category of technical steganography. Whether it is in a keg of beer as in the case of Mary Queen of Scots, the heel of a woman's shoe, or a tattoo on top of a man's head, a good hiding place is almost always a very effective method of steganography.

Microdots

The microdot is a form of microphotography that allows for sheets of printed material to be reduced to a dot that is no larger than 1/2 millimeter across. In 1946, J. Edgar Hoover, then director of the FBI, was quoted as saying that the microdot was the "the enemy's master-piece of espionage," and indeed it has been just that. The microdot has taken on a new form in the modern world and is being used to uniquely identify automobiles and other motor craft. There is even the potential for a microdot to be attached to a strand of DNA.

Computer-Based Methods

With the advancements in computer technologies throughout the 1990s, this is the newest of the steganography methods, and can be very effective in its native environment. There are many computer-based methods, including substitution of bits, addition of bits, and others.

Embedding Methods

The technical challenges of data hiding are formidable. Any "holes" to fill with data in a host signal, either statistical or perceptual, are likely targets for removal by lossy signal compression. The key to successful data hiding is the finding of holes that are not suitable for exploitation by compression algorithms.

Least-Significant Bit (LSB)

Least-significant bit is the substitution method of steganography where the rightmost bit in a binary notation is replaced with a bit from the embedded message. This method provides "security through obscurity," a technique that can be rendered useless if an attacker knows it is being used.

The two most important issues when using LSB substitution is the choice of the image and the choice of the format: 8-, 16-, or 24-bit, compressed or uncompressed.

The cover image first of all must seem casual, so it must be chosen between a set of subjects that can have a reason to be exchanged between the sender and the receiver. The image should have a lot of varying colors; it must be "noisy," so that the added noise is covered by the already present one. Wide solid-color areas show a lot of distortion when even a small amount of noise is added to them. Second, there is a problem with the file size, which involves the choice of the format. Unusually big files exchanged between two peers are likely to cause suspicion.

Most of the experts suggest using 8-bit grayscale images, because their palette is much less varied than the color one, so LSB insertion is very hard to detect by the human eye.

Transform Techniques

There are three main types of transform techniques used when embedding a message in steganography: (1) discrete cosine transform (DCT), (2) discrete Fourier transform, and (3) wavelet transform.

Discrete Cosine Transform (DCT)

The discrete cosine transform, simply put, helps separate the image into parts of differing importance with respect to the image's visual quality. Discrete cosine transform-based image compression relies on two techniques to reduce the data required to represent the image:

1. *Quantization of the image's DCT coefficients.* Quantization is the process of reducing the number of possible values of a quantity, thereby reducing the number of bits needed to represent it.
2. *Entropy coding of the quantized coefficients.* Entropy coding is a technique for representing the quantized data as compactly as possible.

A simple example of quantization is the rounding of real numbers into integers. To represent a real number between 0 and 7 to some specified precision takes many bits. Rounding the number to the nearest integer gives a quantity that can be represented by just three bits.

For example, 2.765423 rounded to 3 takes up fewer bits. By doing this, we can reduce the number of possible values of the quantity, and along with it the number of bits needed to represent it, at the cost of losing information. A "finer" quantization allows for more values and loses less information.

In the JPEG image-compression standard, each cosine transform coefficient is quantized using a weight that depends on the frequencies for that coefficient. The coefficients in each 8 × 8 block are divided by a corresponding entry of an 8 × 8 quantization matrix, and the result is rounded to the nearest integer.

To shed some more light on the DCT, we will take a closer look at how JPEG compression works.

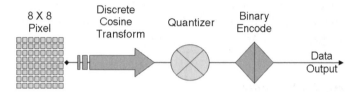

Figure 4.3

1. JPEG divides up the image into 8 × 8 pixel blocks, and then calculates the DCT of each block.
2. The DCT helps separate the image into parts (or spectral sub-bands) of differing importance (with respect to the image's visual quality). In other words, some parts of the image are more important to the overall picture than other parts.
3. A quantizer rounds off the DCT coefficients according to the quantization matrix. At this point it is important to reemphasize that there is a trade-off between image quality and the degree of quantization. A large quantization change can produce unacceptably large image distortion. On the opposite end, finer quantization leads to lower compression ratios. With this said, the question now is how to quantize the DCT coefficients most efficiently. Because of human eyesight's natural high-frequency roll-off, these high frequencies play a less important role than low frequencies. This lets JPEGs make larger modifications to the high frequencies with little noticeable image deterioration. If steganographic data is being loaded into the JPEG image, the loading occurs after this step.
4. This next step produces the "lossy" nature of a JPEG, but this also allows for large compression ratios.
5. JPEG's compression technique uses a variable length code and then writes the compressed data stream to the output file, with the commonly recognized .jpg suffix. During decompression, JPEG recovers the quantized DCT coefficients from the compressed data stream, takes the inverse, and displays the image (Figure 4.3).

The JPEG encoding procedure divides an image into 8 × 8 blocks of pixels. Then they are run through a DCT and the resulting visual frequencies, high and low, are scaled to remove the ones that human viewers would not detect under normal conditions. If steganographic data is going to be loaded into the JPEG, it happens after this step. When this happens, the lowest-order bits of all nonzero frequency coefficients are replaced with the bits from the steganographic source file. These modified coefficients are then sent to the Huffmann coder, which changes color frequencies to a numeric value.

Here is an example showing how steganographic data is encoded:

The steganographic encoding format (the format of data inserted into the lowest-order bits of the image) is as follows:

```
+ — — -+ — — — — — . — — -+ — — — — — — — — — — — — — — — —

    | A | B B B... B | C C C C C C C C C C...

+ — — -+ — — — — — . — — -+ — — — — — — — — — — — — — — — —
```

"A" is 5 bits. It expresses the length (in bits) of field B. Order is most-significant bit first.

"B" is some number of bits from 0 to 31. It expresses the length (in bytes) of the injection file. Order is again most-significant bit first. The range of values for "B" is 0 to 1 billion.

"C" is the bits in the injection file. No ordering is implicit on the bit stream.

This format, by design, makes the steganographic content as inconspicuous as possible. But being inconspicuous is only part of the problem. The storage effectiveness for this technique is decent but not outstanding. Tests have shown that compressing the steganographic file before injecting the message does not greatly harm compression.

Discrete Fourier Transform

The discrete Fourier transform transforms a signal or image from the spatial domain to the frequency domain. Kun-Hung Lee, an engineering student at the University of Bridgeport, creates an excellent analogy for the discrete Fourier transform by comparing how sound frequencies are interpreted by the human ear.

If you used this hypothetical technology to film your eardrum while listening to your best friend saying your name, then took the resulting movie and wrote down the numeric position of your eardrum in every frame of the movie, you would have a digital PCM (pulse code modulation) recording. If you could later make your eardrum move back and forth in accordance with the thousands of numbers you had written down, you would hear your friend's voice saying your name exactly as it sounded the first time. It really does not matter what the sound is — your friend, a crowded party, a symphony. When you hear more than one thing at a time, all the distinct sounds are physically mixed together in your ears as a single pattern of varying air pressure. Your ears and your brain work together to analyze this signal back into separate auditory sensations.

Frequency Information as a Function of Time

An organ in our inner ears called the cochlea enables us to detect tonality in the sounds we hear. The cochlea is acoustically coupled to the eardrum by a series of three tiny bones. It consists of a spiral of tissue filled with liquid and thousands of tiny hairs. The hairs on the outside of the spiral are longer than the hairs on the inside of the spiral. Each hair is connected to a nerve that feeds into the auditory nerve bundle going to the brain. The longer hairs resonate with lower frequency sounds, and the shorter hairs with higher frequencies. Thus the cochlea serves to transform the air pressure signal experienced by the eardrum into frequency information that can be interpreted by the brain as tonality and texture. This way, we can tell the difference between adjacent notes on a piano, even if they are played equally loud. The Fourier transform is another mathematical technique for doing a similar thing: resolving any time-domain function into a frequency spectrum, much like a prism splitting light into a spectrum of colors. This analogy is not perfect, but it gets the basic idea across.

There is another transform technique that you may come across if you delve deeper into the mathematics of steganography called the wavelet transform, which is very similar in concept to the Fourier transform.

Spread-Spectrum Encoding

Spread-spectrum encoding is the method of hiding a small or narrowband signal, a message, in a larger cover signal. The foundation of this process begins with a spread-spectrum encoder. The encoder works by modulating a narrowband signal over a carrier. The carrier signal is continually shifted using a noise generator and a secret key that makes the noise seem random. The message is embedded in the existing noise of the carrier signal, spreading the narrow signal over a wide area. This decreases the density of the hidden signal and makes it much more difficult to detect within the overall carrier signal.

Spread-spectrum encoding allows for very high data rates because messages can be compressed before being encoded in the carrier signal. Redundant data can also be added to the signal for error correction. Spread-spectrum is usually very robust because the addition of noise does not usually destroy the message. However, it is possible to remove the message with noise reduction filters, which would be used by the intended recipient to extract the message.

Spread-spectrum encoding is a very good method of steganography because of its difficulty to detect; if it is detected, it is usually more difficult to decipher because the attacker would also need the secret key used to encode the message.

Perceptual Masking

This form of steganography occurs when one signal or sound becomes imperceptible to the observer because of the presence of another signal. This method also exploits the weaknesses of the human visual and auditory systems. A common example that almost everyone has seen is in spy films where someone is trying to communicate with someone else in a room they know is bugged. Usually the secret agent will turn up the stereo, run the shower, or do some other innocent (but noisy) task that allows a whispered conversation to take place without being heard.

Steganography Applied to Different Media

Still Images

The methods of steganography are quite varied; in still images, least-significant bit insertion and spread-spectrum techniques are used.

Texture block uses low bit-rate data hiding, and is accomplished by copying a region from a random texture pattern in a picture to an area of similar texture, resulting in a pair of identically textured regions in a picture.

Patchwork uses a low bit-rate data hiding based on a pseudorandom, statistical process. Patchwork invisibly embeds in a host image a specific statistic, and takes two places within a picture and lightens one and darkens the other.

Other methods include dithering manipulation, perceptual masking, and DCT coefficients manipulation.

Moving Images

Steganography, when applied to a video file such as an .avi or .mpeg, typically uses discrete cosine transform (DCT) manipulation. Westfeld and Wolf have described a method for data hiding in a videoconferencing system. Because videoconferencing needs to have a high frame rate on often narrow-band digital networks, DCT manipulation is a necessary and valuable part of the process. Basically, videoconferencing applications compress each frame with "differential lossy compression," meaning only the differences between successive stills are compressed, then broadcast. This renders the embedding technique almost invisible. While differences between an original and a stego-image can be detected, it is likely that no one can tell which is which. Because the videoconferencing system would broadcast only the differences between successive frames, the threat of detection by comparison between successive similar frames would not be a factor. Other attacks are equally unlikely to succeed in detecting or extracting the stego-message. Added noise would be very similar to the original noise and the data would be embedded before encryption, making it that much more difficult to find. The data rate for this technique could be as high as 8 kbps if embedded into an ISDN videoconference. This technique could be a very valuable and effective steganography method due to a high data rate and ease of stealth.

Audio Files

When developing data-hiding methods for audio, the first consideration is the most likely environment the sound signal will travel between encoding and decoding. There are two main areas of modification that we will consider: first, the storage environment, or digital representation of the signal, and second, the transmission pathway the signal might travel.

There are several methods for adding steganographic information to audio files:

1. The high bit-rate LSB insertion is easily destroyed by anything other than a pure digital transmission.
2. Differential phase variation, which is based on the sensitivity of the human auditory system. The human ear is sensitive to differential phase variation, but is relatively insensitive to the initial phase. The sound file is divided into blocks and each block's initial phase is modified using the embedded message. This preserves

the subsequent phase shifts, meaning less differences, and therefore harder for the ear to detect. This technique is very good when dealing with perceived signal-to-noise ratio.

Phase coding works by substituting the phase of an initial audio segment with a reference phase. The reference phase represents the data. The phase of all the following segments is adjusted to preserve the relative phase between segments while allowing data to be embedded. Phase coding is one of the most effective coding methods when it comes to signal-to-perceived noise ratio.

Absolute phases can withstand a fair amount of modification; however, if the relative phase differences between the blocks is preserved, the ear will be less likely to detect any changes. As long as phase modification is small, inaudible coding can be achieved.

3. Spread spectrum can be used a couple of ways. It has the ability to stay effective even if perceivable noise is added to the sound; and while adding noise is possible, the embedded signal can be filtered through a perceptual mask. To eliminate this problem, often the most audible components of the added noise are reduced in power. Then there is the basic spread-spectrum technique, which is designed to encode a stream of information by spreading the data across as much of the frequency spectrum as possible. This allows for signal reception, even if there is interference.

4. Adding echo to the audio signal. Echo hiding is a robust and high data-rate method of embedding information into an audio signal. Adding an echo uses two different delays to encode the bits. They are both small enough to be heard with the naked ear, but they are perceived as something that enriches the sound rather than distorts it. This method is the only one that can resist a jitter attack. When adding echo, the data is hidden by varying initial amplitude, decay rate, and offset.

When the delay between the original sound and the echo decreases, the signals blend and the human ear cannot distinguish between the two. Information is embedded by echoing the original signal with one of two delay kernels. A binary one is represented by an echo kernel with a change plus one-second delay. A binary zero is represented by a change plus zero-second delay. The extraction of the embedded information involves detecting the spaces between the echoes.

Using this method you can see it is possible to encode and decode information with minimal alteration of the original audio signal. Minimal alteration means the signal has been changed in such a way that the average human cannot hear any significant difference between the original and altered signal. If there is an alteration, it actually works in the encoder's favor by giving the signal a richer sound.

Text Files

Open-Space Method

The open-space method uses white space on the printed page.

1. *Inter-sentence spacing:* Encodes a binary message by placing one or two spaces after each terminating character (period or semicolon). The problem with this method is that it is very inefficient as it requires a lot of space for a small message, and inconsistent use of white space is easily spotted.
2. *End-of-line spacing:* Data is inserted in the form of spaces at the end of a line. This allows for much more room to insert a message, but can present problems if a program automatically removes extra spaces or the document is turned into hard copy.
3. *Inter-word spacing:* Uses right justification. The justification spaces are adjusted to allow for binary encoding. One space between words is a 0, two spaces are a 1. Open space works as long as text remains ASCII.

Syntactic Method

Deriving from "syntax," this method uses the manipulation of punctuation to hide information. Syntactic is a method that utilizes punctuations and contradictions. For example:

```
bread, cereal, and milk
bread, cereal and milk
```

Semantic Method

A final category of data hiding in text involves changing the words themselves. Semantic methods are similar to the syntactic method. Rather than encoding binary data by exploiting ambiguity of form, these methods assign two synonyms primary or secondary value. For example, the word "big" could be considered primary and "large" secondary. Whether a word has primary or secondary value bears no relevance to how often it will be used, but primary words will be read as ones, secondary words as zeros when decoding.

Steganographic File Systems

A steganographic file system is a method of storing files that encrypts data and hides it so that it cannot be proven to be there. A steganographic file system can:

- Hide users' documents in other, seemingly random files.
- Allow the owner to give names and passwords for some files while keeping others secret.
- Provide a second layer of secrecy. Encrypted files are out in the open and visible but not understandable. Stego files are not even visible and an outsider cannot look for files that "are not there."

A stego file system can protect from some threats:

- Torture to reveal crypto keys or other secrets.
- When conducting delicate negotiations, such as between a company and a trade union, informal offers may be made, which will be denied in the event of later litigation. However, the other side might obtain court orders for access to documents.

To elaborate on this concept, for example, a user of a steganographic file system is put in a position to reveal three different passwords used to protect different directories with his or her e-mail archive, tax records, and love letters, but keeps quiet about the directory containing his or her trade secrets. The person who is getting these passwords would have no way of proving that such a directory exists.

The classical way of hiding information in a deniable way would be to use a steganographic program to embed the information in large files such as audio or video, although there are some problems with this approach:

- One can only hide so much information before its presence becomes noticeable. If an opponent is allowed to subject these objects to small distortions of his or her choice, then the usable bandwidth can be very low indeed.
- The goal has always been to design a practical steganographic system, meaning that normal UNIX or Windows applications can

run on it. Because any manual method of file recovery would become very inconvenient, and subsequently not used to the extent it could be, a high degree of transparency is best.

Steganographic file systems are designed to overcome the drawbacks of using individual files for hiding information. A stego file system aims to create a secure file system where the risk of users being forced to reveal private data is eliminated by giving the users the ability to truthfully say that there is no encrypted data hiding on the disk. Following is a discussion of the two ways of constructing a stego file system.

Method #1

- The program operates using a set of cover files with initially random content.
- Data files are stored by modifying the cover files.
- The number of cover files must be sufficiently large to guarantee that trying all subsets of cover files remains computationally infeasible.

Problems

- A lot of cover files would have to be read and authenticated to ensure security.
- The prospect of low performance for both read and write access.

Method #2

- The file system starts out being full of completely random data.
- The file blocks are hidden within this random data by writing the encrypted blocks to pseudo-random locations using a key derived from the file name and directory password, making the file blocks indistinguishable from the random data.
- As blocks continue to be written to the file system, collisions will occur and blocks will be overwritten, meaning only a small proportion of the disk space could safely be utilized.
- Multiple copies of each block would have to be written.
- A method to identify blocks when they have been overwritten would also be needed.

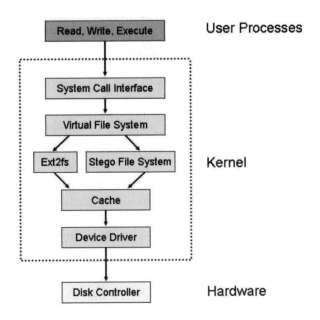

Figure 4.4

Stego File System Construction

In this explanation, the stego file system design is based on the second method of construction because it is more practical and efficient. This system does not use a separate partition of a hard disk, but instead places hidden files into unused blocks of a partition that also contains normal files, managed under a standard file system.

- Stego file system (StegFS) partitions are compatible with Ext2fs partitions, meaning drivers for both file systems will work with each other. This feature lets the StegFS partition look like a partition that has recently been overwritten with random bytes using some disk-wiping tool.
- StegFS can store hidden files in the blocks that are currently unused by Ext2fs, except that when files are deleted, their blocks will be overwritten with random bytes.
- A small fraction of the newly created files are placed at a somewhat more random location on the disk than normal to help simulate normal use (Figure 4.4).

This has shown a practical implementation of a steganographic file system. It offers the following functionality:

- Users can plausibly deny certain files being stored on the disk.
- Guaranteed confidentiality of hidden files.
- The deletion of hidden and nonhidden files ensures secure destruction.
- Layers of security can be used, ensuring that the compromise of lower layers does not reveal the presence of higher ones.
- Deniability of the existence of higher layers.
- The installation of the driver can be justified by the additional security advantages it provides.
- Write accesses that are performed while not all hidden layers are open are unlikely to damage data in hidden files.
- Write access to hidden files between inspections cannot be distinguished from nonhidden files that have been created or deleted.
- Nonhidden files are accessible when the StegFS driver and its block allocation table are temporarily removed.
- The full UNIX file system semantics are implemented.

Hiding in Disk Space

In this section we will discuss three different methods for hiding information steganographically in disk space: S-tools, hidden partitions, and slack space.

S-Tools

Similar to the method used in the stego file system, S-Tools will spread the file bits out throughout the free space on the floppy. This is undetectable in the normal Windows viewer, but the file is there.

S-Tools Version 3 has the ability to embed information in unused tracks of a floppy disk. While this program is not widely available on the Internet these days, it is still possible to find it and you may encounter this particular function.

How It Is Done

S-Tools will allow you to hide files in the unused space on floppy disks. To understand what is meant by unused space, look at the way DOS organizes the files on a disk. Every floppy disk, when formatted, is divided into sectors. Each sector on a disk can hold 512 bytes of information. On a 1.44 Mb disk, there are $1440 \times 1024/512 = 2880$ sectors. When you write a file to the disk, DOS computes how many sectors it will need to hold the file and writes this information into the file allocation table (FAT).

S-Tools' FDD (feature-driven development) module will look at the FAT to decide which disk sectors have not been used, and will allow you to hide information on them. S-Tools will not hide information in consecutive sectors on disk because this would be too easy to detect. Instead it uses a random number generator to choose which free sectors to use. S-Tools will add additional security by allowing you to fill all other unused sectors on the disk with random data.

Using This Module

There are a few tips that you might want to be aware of when using the FDD module. If you want to be able to plausibly deny having any concealed data on your disks, it would make sense to fill the unused space on all your newly formatted disks with random data. This way any concealed data will appear to be "lost in the noise."

One point to remember with this feature of S-Tools: Do not write any ordinary files to the disk after you have concealed information on it. Depending on the amount of space you have left on the disk, it is very likely that DOS will overwrite your hidden information. This point can also work in your favor because there may be a situation where you want the hidden information destroyed.

Analyze Disk

This option displays a usage map of the floppy and tells you how much information you can hide on it. S-Tools will work with any capacity of disk that DOS can use, up to a maximum of 1.44 Mb. Sectors marked in red are the ones that S-Tools cannot use because files are already stored there. The status bar at the bottom of the screen will tell you how much information you can hide on the disk (Figure 4.5 through Figure 4.7).

Fill Free Space

This option allows you to fill the unused sectors on a disk with random data. This will mask the presence of any file that you want to hide on the disk. S-Tools automatically asks you whether you want to fill the free space after hiding a file.

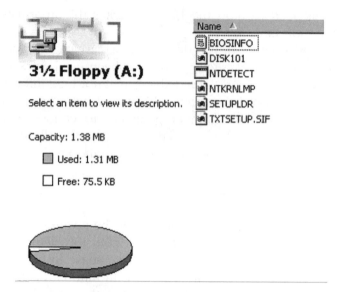

Figure 4.5

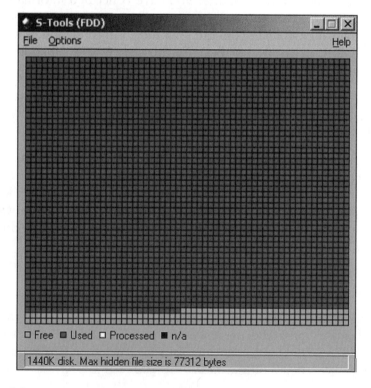

Figure 4.6

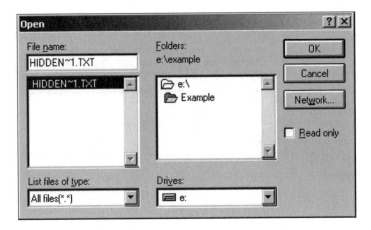

Figure 4.7

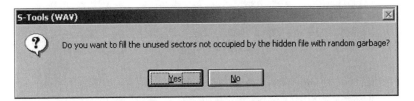

Figure 4.8

A Word of Warning

If you fill the free space on a disk *after* hiding a file, you will lose that file. After hiding, S-Tools will forget about its presence until you use the reveal operation. If at any time you decide you want to stop the process, hit the Escape key (Figure 4.8).

Hide File

This is the option that you use when you want to hide a file on disk. If you are not sure whether the disk has enough free space to hold the hidden file, then you can use the Analyze Disk option to find out.

First you are asked to choose the file that you want to hide. If you have asked to be prompted for encryption options, you will be asked whether the file should be encrypted before hiding. Using encryption is recommended even if the file is already encrypted because the pass phrase that you enter is also used to seed the random number generator

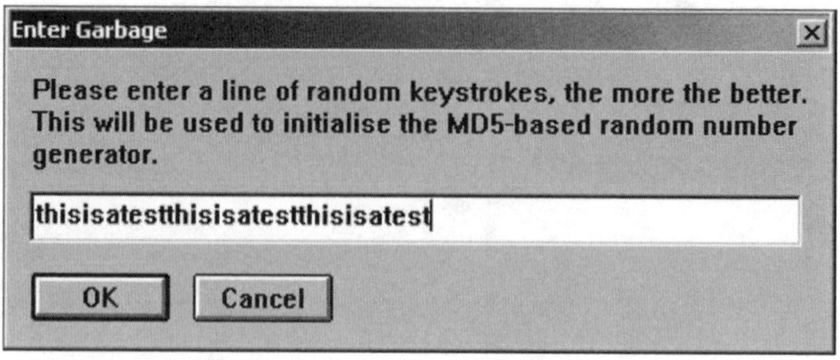

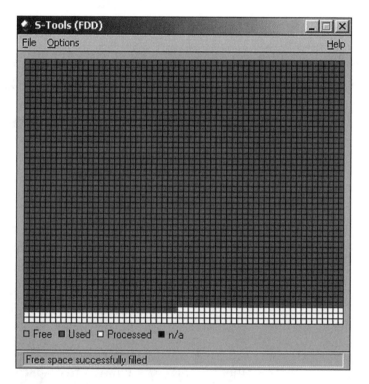

Figure 4.9

Figure 4.10

that is used to choose the sectors that will hold the hidden file. Again, if you want to cancel the operation press the Escape key (Figure 4.9 through Figure 4.11).

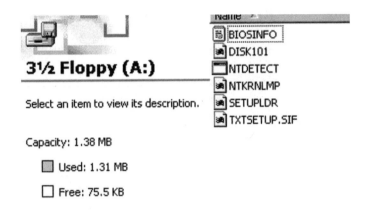

3½ Floppy (A:)

Select an item to view its description.

Capacity: 1.38 MB

☐ Used: 1.31 MB

☐ Free: 75.5 KB

Figure 4.11

Reveal File

This is the option that you should use to reveal a file that has been hidden on a disk. Simply insert the disk into the disk drive and select this option. If encryption was selected as an option when the file was embedded, then you must supply the correct pass phrase in order to reveal it. If everything works as planned, S-Tools will look at the disk and decide whether a file is hidden on it. If there is a hidden file, the program will tell you the size of the file and give you the option of viewing it or saving it.

Hidden Partitions

A hidden partition on a hard drive is another way of hiding large amounts of information in plain sight. The simplest explanation is a Linux partition chock full of secret messages hiding on a hard drive with only a Windows operating system. While this likely would not fool someone who was actively looking for hidden information, it would fool a casual user or someone unfamiliar with the computer's setup.

Slack Space

Slack space is the unused space in a disk. Even if the actual data being stored requires less storage than the cluster size, an entire cluster is reserved for the file. The unused space is called the slack space.

For example, the minimum space allocated on the hard drive is 32 kb and we have a file that is 6 kb. This leaves 26 kb unused and considered unavailable by the operating system. This unused space, slack space, could be used to hide information without showing up in any directory or file system.

Hiding in Network Packets

A covert channel is described as "any communication channel that can be exploited by a process to transfer information in a manner that violates the system's security policy." Essentially, it is a method of communication that is not part of an actual computer system design, but can be used to transfer information to users or system processes that normally would not be allowed access to the information.

In TCP/IP, there are a number of methods available whereby covert channels can be established and data can be surreptitiously passed between hosts.

This method can be used in a variety of areas:

- Bypassing packet filters, network sniffers, and "dirty word" search engines
- Encapsulating encrypted or nonencrypted information within otherwise normal packets of information for secret transmission through networks that prohibit such activity ("TCP/IP steganography")
- Concealing locations of transmitted data by "bouncing" forged packets with encapsulated information off innocuous Internet sites

Background Terminology

For our purposes, it is important to realize that TCP is a "connection-oriented" or "reliable" protocol. Simply put, TCP has certain features that ensure data arrives at the remote host in an intact manner (usually). The basic operation of this relies on the initial TCP "three-way handshake":

- *Step One:* Send a synchronize (SYN) packet and Initial Sequence Number (ISN). Host A wishes to establish a connection to Host B. Host A sends a solitary packet to Host B with the synchronize bit (SYN) set announcing the new connection and an Initial Sequence Number (ISN), which will allow tracking of packets sent between hosts:

Host A — — — SYN(ISN) — — — > Host B

- *Step Two:* Allow remote host to respond with an acknowledgment (ACK). Host B responds to the request by sending a packet with the synchronize bit set (SYN) and ACK (acknowledgment) bit set in the packet back to the calling host. This packet contains not only the responding client's own sequence number, but the Initial Sequence Number plus one (ISN + 1) to indicate the remote packet was correctly received as part of the acknowledgment and is awaiting the next transmission:

Host A < — — — — SYN(ISN+1)/ACK — — — — Host B

- *Step Three:* Complete negotiation by sending a final acknowledgment to the remote host. At this point Host A sends back a final ACK packet and sequence number to indicate successful reception; the connection is complete and data can now flow:

Host A — — — ACK — — — > Host B

The entire connection process happens in a matter of milliseconds, and each packet from this point on is independently acknowledged by both sides. This handshake method ensures a reliable connection between hosts and is why TCP is considered a connection-oriented protocol. It should be noted that only TCP packets exhibit this negotiation process. This is not so with UDP packets, which are considered unreliable and do not attempt to correct errors nor negotiate a connection before sending to a remote host. This chapter deals with the TCP protocol primarily to exploit the acknowledgment feature, which will be described next. The thrust of these methods, however, could be easily supported on the UDP protocol type.

Encoding Information in a TCP/IP Header

Within each header, there are several areas that are not used for normal transmission or are "optional" fields to be set as needed by the sender of the datagrams.

An analysis of the areas of a typical IP header that are either unused or optional reveals many possibilities where data can be stored and transmitted (Figure 4.12 and Figure 4.13).

For our purposes, we will focus on encapsulation of data in the more mandatory fields. This is not because they are any better than

```
0            4            8          16   19        24          32

----------------------------------------------------------------------
| VERS |  HLEN |    Service Type    |          Total Length           |
----------------------------------------------------------------------
|          Identification           | Flags |      Fragment Offset    |
----------------------------------------------------------------------
|                       Source IP Address                             |
----------------------------------------------------------------------
|                     Destination IP Address                          |
----------------------------------------------------------------------
|                          IP Options              |   Padding        |
----------------------------------------------------------------------
|                             Data                                    |
----------------------------------------------------------------------
```

Figure 4.12

```
0           4            8          16  19  24                   32

----------------------------------------------------------------------
|          Source Port             |         Destination Port         |
----------------------------------------------------------------------
|                        Sequence Number                              |
----------------------------------------------------------------------
|                     Acknowledgment Number                           |
----------------------------------------------------------------------
| HLEN |  Reserved |   Code Bits    |          Window                 |
----------------------------------------------------------------------
|          Checksum                |        Urgent Pointer            |
----------------------------------------------------------------------
|                              Options     |      Padding             |
----------------------------------------------------------------------
|                             Data                                    |
----------------------------------------------------------------------|
```

Figure 4.13

the other optional areas; rather, these fields are not as likely to be altered in transit as the IP or TCP options fields, which are sometimes changed or stripped off by packet-filtering mechanisms or through fragment reassembly.

Rowland excellently describes three methods of adding information in his article, "Covert Channels in the TCP/IP Protocol Suite."* He describes encode and decode in the following fields:

- The IP packet identification field
- The TCP initial sequence number field
- The TCP acknowledged sequence number field

Method One: Manipulation of the IP Identification Field

The identification field of the IP Protocol helps with reassembly of packet data by remote routers and host systems. Its purpose is to give a unique value to packets so that if fragmentation occurs along a route, they can be accurately reassembled. The first encoding method simply replaces the IP identification field with the numerical ASCII representation of the character to be encoded. This allows for easy transmission to a remote host, which simply reads the IP identification field and translates the encoded ASCII value to its printable counterpart. The lines below show a tcpdump representation of the packets on a network between two hosts, "nemesis.psionic.com" and "blast.psionic.com." A coded message consisting of the letters H-E-L-L-O was sent between the two hosts in packets appearing to be destined for the Web server on blast.psionic.com. The actual packet data does not matter.

The field in question is the IP portion of the packet, called the ID field, located in the parentheses. Note that the ID field is represented by an unsigned integer during the packet generation process of the included program. This program does not perform any type of byte-ordering functions normally used in this process; therefore, packet data is converted to the ASCII equivalent by dividing by 256.

> Packet One:
> 18:50:13.551117 nemesis.psionic.com.7180 >
> blast.psionic.com.www: S 537657344:537657344(0) win 512
> (ttl 64, id 18432)
> Decoding: ... (ttl 64, id 18432/256) [ASCII: 72(H)]

---

* Available at www.firstmonday.dk/issues/issue2_5/rowland/#dep2

Packet Two:

    18:50:14.551117 nemesis.psionic.com.51727 >
    blast.psionic.com.www: S1393295360:1393295360(0) win 512
    (ttl 64, id 17664)
    Decoding: ... (ttl 64, id 17664/256) [ASCII: 69(E)]

Packet Three:

    18:50:15.551117 nemesis.psionic.com.9473 >
    blast.psionic.com.www: S 3994419200:3994419200(0) win 512
    (ttl 64, id 19456)
    Decoding: ... (ttl 64, id 19456/256) [ASCII: 76(L)]

Packet Four:

    18:50:16.551117 nemesis.psionic.com.56855 >
    blast.psionic.com.www: S3676635136:3676635136(0) win 512
    (ttl 64, id 19456)
    Decoding: ... (ttl 64, id 19456/256) [ASCII: 76(L)]

Packet Five:

    18:50:17.551117 nemesis.psionic.com.1280 >
    blast.psionic.com.www: S 774242304:774242304(0) win 512
    (ttl 64, id 20224)
    Decoding: ... (ttl 64, id 20224/256) [ASCII: 79(O)]

Packet Six:

    18:50:18.551117 nemesis.psionic.com.21004 >
    blast.psionic.com.www: S3843751936:3843751936(0) win 512
    (ttl 64, id 2560)
    Decoding: ... (ttl 64, id 2560/256) [ASCII: 10(Carriage Return)]

This method is used by having the client host construct a packet with the appropriate destination host and source host information and encoded IP ID field. This packet is sent to the remote host, which is listening on a passive socket that decodes the data. This method is relatively straightforward and easy to implement, as shown in the included covert_tcp program. You should note that this method relies on manipulation of the IP header information, and may be more susceptible to packet filtering and network address translation where the header information may be rewritten in transit, especially if located behind a firewall. If this happens, loss of the encoded data may occur.

Method Two: Initial Sequence Number Field

The Initial Sequence Number field (ISN) of the TCP/IP Protocol suite enables a client to establish a reliable protocol negotiation with a remote server. As part of the negotiation process for TCP/IP, several steps are taken in what is commonly called a "three-way handshake," as described earlier. For our purposes, the sequence number field serves as a perfect medium for transmitting clandestine data because of its size (a 32-bit number). In this light, there are a number of possible methods to use. The simplest is to generate the sequence number from the actual ASCII character we wish to have encoded. This is the method used by covert_tcp, as shown in the following packets. (The "S" indicates a synchronize packet; the ten-digit number following is the sequence number being sent.) Again, no byte-ordering functions are used by covert_tcp to generate the sequence numbers. This enables a more realistic looking sequence number. Therefore, in our example the sequence numbers are converted to ASCII by dividing by 16777216, which is a representation of 65536 × 256. Again, our message of H-E-L-L-O is being sent:

 Packet One:
  18:50:29.071117 nemesis.psionic.com.45321 >
  blast.psionic.com.www: S 1207959552:1207959552(0) win 512
  (ttl 64, id 49408)
  Decoding: ... S 1207959552/16777216 [ASCII: 72(H)]
 Packet Two:
  18:50:30.071117 nemesis.psionic.com.65292 >
  blast.psionic.com.www: S 1157627904:1157627904(0) win 512
  (ttl 64, id 47616)
  Decoding: ... S 1157627904/16777216 [ASCII: 69(E)]
 Packet Three:
  18:50:31.071117 nemesis.psionic.com.25120 >
  blast.psionic.com.www: S 1275068416:1275068416(0) win 512
  (ttl 64, id 41984)
  Decoding: ... S 1275068416/16777216 [ASCII: 76(L)]
 Packet Four:
  18:50:32.071117 nemesis.psionic.com.13603 >
  blast.psionic.com.www: S 1275068416:1275068416(0) win 512
  (ttl 64, id 7936)
  Decoding: ... S 1275068416/16777216 [ASCII: 76(L)]
 Packet Five:
  18:50:33.071117 nemesis.psionic.com.45830 >
  blast.psionic.com.www: S 1325400064:1325400064(0) win 512
  (ttl 64, id 3072)
  Decoding: ... S 1325400064/16777216 [ASCII: 79(O)]

Packet Six:
18:50:34.071117 nemesis.psionic.com.64535 >
blast.psionic.com.www: S 167772160:167772160(0) win 512
(ttl 64, id 54528)
Decoding: ... S 167772160/16777216 [ASCII: 10(Carriage
Return)]

Using this method, the packet is constructed with the appropriate data in the SYN field and sent to the destination host. The destination host, expecting to receive information from the client, simply grabs the SYN field of each incoming packet to reconstruct the encoded data. This is done with a passive listening socket on the remote end, as described earlier.

Because of the sheer amount of information one can represent in a 32-bit address space (4,294,967,296 numbers), the sequence number makes an ideal location for storing data. Aside from the obvious example given previously, one can use a number of other techniques to store information in either a byte fashion or as bits of information represented through careful manipulation of the sequence number. The simple algorithm of the covert_tcp program takes the ASCII value of our data and converts it to a usable sequence number (which is actually done by the packet generation functions and is converted back to ASCII in a symmetrical manner). Note that this method is similar to a "substitution cipher," whereby packets containing the same information will display the same sequence number (note packets three and four, which contain the letter "L" in the encoding and their sequence numbers). Methods that incorporate a random number generation of the sequence number with a subsequent inclusion of the data to be encoded through an XOR or similar operation may yield a more random result. Inclusion of encrypted data to perform the same function is a logical extension of this idea.

Method Three: The TCP Acknowledge Sequence Number Field "Bounce"

This method relies on basic spoofing of IP addresses to enable a sending machine to "bounce" a packet of information off a remote site and have that site return the packet to the real destination address. This has the benefit of concealing the sender of the packet, as it appears to come from the "bounce" host. This method could be used to set up an anonymous one-way communication network that would be difficult to detect, especially if the bounce server is very busy.

This method relies on the characteristic of TCP/IP where the destination server responds to an initial connect request (SYN packet) with a SYN/ACK packet containing the original initial sequence number plus one (ISN + 1). In this method, the sender constructs a packet that contains the following information:

- Forged SOURCE IP address
- Forged SOURCE port
- Forged DESTINATION IP address
- Forged DESTINATION port
- TCP SYN number with encoded data

The source and destination ports chosen do not matter (except if you want to conceal the traffic as a well-known service such as HTTP, and you are having the receiving server listening for data on a predetermined port, in which case you will want to forge the source port as well). The DESTINATION IP address should be the server you wish to *bounce* information off of and the SOURCE IP should be the address of the server you wish to *communicate with*.

The packet is sent from the client's computer system and routed to the forged destination IP address in the header ("bounce server"). The bounce server receives the packet and sends either a SYN/ACK or a SYN/RST, depending on the state of the port the packet was destined for on the bounce server. The return packet is sent to the forged source address with the ISN number plus one. The listening destination server takes this incoming packet and decodes the information by transforming the returned sequence number minus one back into the ASCII equivalent. It should be noted that the low-order bits are dropped in the translation process of covert_tcp because of the method used to "encode" and "decode" information, so the program does not need to adjust for the incremented SYN packet number.

Following is a step-by-step representation of the bounce method:

Sending Client: A
Bounce Server: B
Receiving Server: C

- *Step One:* Client A sends a forged packet with encoded information to bounce server B. This packet has the address of receiving server C.
- *Step Two:* Bounce server B receives the packet and returns an appropriate SYN/ACK or SYN/RST packet based on the status of

the port. Because bounce server B thinks the packet came from receiving server C, the packet is sent to the address of receiving server C. The acknowledgment sequence number (which is the encoded sequence number plus one) is sent to server C as well.

■ *Step Three:* Server C, expecting to receive a packet from bounce server B (or a predetermined port) decodes the data and writes it out to disk.

This method is essentially tricking the remote server into sending the packet and encapsulated data back to the forged source IP address, which it rightfully thinks is legitimate. From the receiving end, the packet appears to originate from the bounce server, and indeed it does. As a side note, if the receiving system is behind a packet filter that allows communication only to certain sites, this method can be used to bounce packets off the trusted sites; this will then relay them to the system behind the packet filter with a legitimate source address. This could be vital in communicating with receiving servers in heavily protected or scrutinized networks.

Bouncing a packet off a well-known Internet site (.mil, .gov, .com, etc.) is also a useful technique for concealing operations in ordinary traffic. Be sure the bounce site is not using round-robin DNS (stable IP address) or, if it is, that the receiving server is passively listening on a predetermined port to decode the transmissions from multiple sites (i.e., send out a forged source address and source port of 1234 so the bounce server returns the packet to the listening server on port 1234). Using this technique, the sending client can bounce packets off hundreds of Internet hosts while the receiving server listens and writes out any data destined for the predefined port number regardless of IP address.

If your network site has a correctly configured router, it may not allow a forged packet with a network number that is not from its network to traverse outbound. Alas, many routers are not configured with this protection in mind and will happily pass the data, so you can generally expect this technique to work.

Implications, Protection, and Detection

The implications of these methods depend on the intent and purposes they are being used for. This method of covert channel could be used immediately as an alternative to encryption in countries that have a stricter stance on cryptography, such as China and France. Additionally, this technique could be used quite effectively for data smuggling and anonymous communication.

Protection from this technique would start with the use of an application proxy firewall system. An application proxy firewall is designed to keep packets from logically separated networks from passing directly to each other. A packet-filter firewall is another option, but is not as effective as the application proxy firewall.

Detection of these techniques can be difficult. If the information in the packet data is encrypted or is "bounced" from another server, it can be very difficult to determine where the packet originated. One way to determine where a forged packet originated is to put a sniffer on the inbound side of the server.

Issues in Information Hiding

Levels of Visibility

When looking at the first issue in information hiding, determining levels of visibility can be done by asking one question: Does the embedding process distort the cover to the point where it is visually noticeable? If the image is unacceptably distorted, the carrier is not sufficient for the payload; if it is not distorted, the carrier is enough.

Robustness Versus Payload

Most things in life require trade-offs of some sort. Something for nothing is not the way the universe works, and information hiding is no different. To have a robust method of embedding the message means you must have redundancy to resist changes made to the cover. This redundancy subsequently lowers the payload.

The exact opposite is also true. With little or no redundancy (robustness) the payload of the secret message can be larger.

- More robust = lower payload
- Less robust = higher payload

File Format Dependence

Some image and sound files are either lossy or lossless; the conversion of lossless information to the compressed "lossy" information can

Stego Medium

Figure 4.14

destroy the hidden information in the cover. A good example is to think of the conversion of an uncompressed bitmap to a compressed, estimated JPEG. The compression and estimation change the bits to include the bits that might be the embedded message.

Attacks

- *Stego-only attack:* Attack is one where we only have the stego-medium, and we want to detect and extract the embedded message (Figure 4.14).
- *Known-cover attack:* Attack is used when we have both the stego-medium and the cover-medium, so that a comparison can be made between the two (Figure 4.15).

Cover Medium

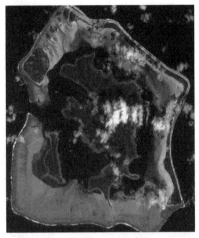

Hash value:
A2F53479JG4FNB621354CD67TG679912

Stego Medium

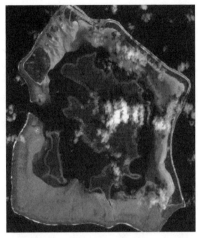

Hash value:
CR34I479JG4FNYT462A4CD67TG678UT6

Figure 4.15

- *Known-message attack:* Attack assumes that we know the message and the stego-medium, and we want to find the method used for embedding the message (Figure 4.16).
- *Chosen-stego attack:* Attack is used when we have both the stego-medium and the steganography tool or algorithm (Figure 4.17).
- *Chosen-message attack:* Attack is one where the steganalyst generates a stego-medium from a message using a particular tool, looking for signatures that will enable the detection of other stego-media. (Figure 4.18).

Disabling Information

We have seen, through steganalysis, that we can detect the existence of hidden information, thereby defeating the imperceptibility that steganography tries to maintain. However, there are methods other than detection that are much more effective. These methods are called active attacks and rather than try to detect hidden information, their purpose is to destroy it. The primary advantage of using active over passive attacks is that they are easier to implement because it is easier to

Message

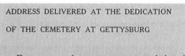

Stego Medium

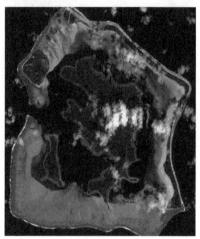

Figure 4.16

Stego Medium

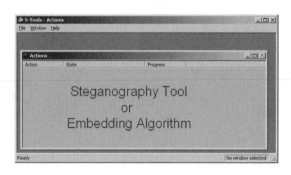

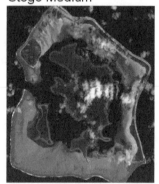

Figure 4.17

destroy than detect. Following are some active attack methods and their descriptions.

■ *Blur:* Smoothes transitions and decreases contrast by averaging the pixels next to the hard edges of defined lines and areas where there are significant color transitions.

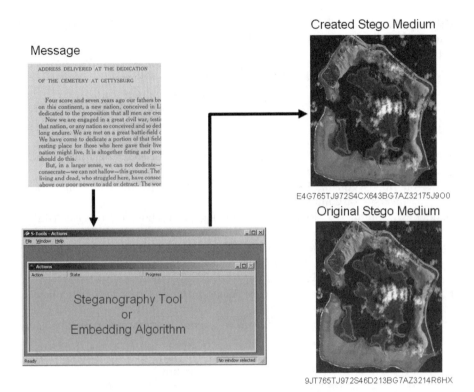

Figure 4.18

- *Noise:* Random noise inserts random-colored pixels to an image. Uniform noise inserts pixels and colors that closely resemble the original pixels.
- *Noise reduction:* Reduces noise in the image by adjusting the colors and averaging pixel values.
- *Sharpen:* Sharpening is the opposite of blur. It increases contrast between adjacent pixels where there are significant color contrasts, usually at the edge of objects.
- *Rotate:* Rotation moves an image around its center point in a given plane.
- *Resample:* Resampling involves an interpolation process to minimize the "raggedness" normally associated with expanding an image.
- *Soften:* Applies a uniform blur to an image to smooth edges and reduce contrasts, and causes less distortion than blurring.

With all of these ways to disable hidden information, how does steganography stand up to these types of active attacks? The simple truth is it does not, especially when more than one is applied in succession, as is the case with the StirMark tool. Watermarking tools, which do not have to work at secrecy, tend to fare much better but are still subject to being damaged by these attacks.

Bibliography

Anderson, R.J. and Petitcolas, F.A.P., "On the Limits of Steganography," *IEEE J. Selected Areas Commun.*, May, 1998.

Anderson, R., Needham, R., and Shamir, A., *The Steganographic File System,* University of Cambridge.

Bender, W., Gruhl, D., Morimoto, N., and Lu, A., Techniques for Data Hiding, *IBM Systems Journal,* 35, 3 and 4, 1996.

Chapman, M.T., *Hiding the Hidden: A Software System for Concealing Ciphertext as Innocuous Text,* First International Conference, Information and Communication Security, 1997.

Fortini, M., *Steganography and Digital Watermarking: A Global View,* University of California, Davis.

Fridrich, J., *Applications of Hiding Data in Digital Images,* Center for Intelligent Systems, 1998.

Johnson, N.F., *Steganography and Digital Watermarking: Information Hiding,* available at http://www.jjtc.com/Steganography/.

Judge, J.C., *Steganography: Past, Present, and Future,* SANS, 2001.

Katzenbeisser, S. and Petitcolas, F.A.P., (Eds.), *Information Hiding: Techniques for Steganography and Watermarking,* Artech House, Boston, 2000.

Lee, K-H, *An Application of Discrete Fast Fourier Transform Algorithm,* available at http://www.bridgeport.edu/sed/projects/cs597/Summer_2002/ kunhlee/, University of Bridgeport, 2002.

Lin, E.T. and Delp, E.J., *A Review of Data Hiding in Digital Images,* Purdue University.

Marvel, L.M., Boncelet, C.G., Jr., and Retter, C.T., "Reliable Blind Information for Hiding Images," International Workshop for Information Hiding, April, 1998.

McDonald, A.D. and Kuhn, M.G., *StegFS: A Steganographic File System for Linux,* University of Cambridge, Computer Laboratory, U.K.

Rabinovich, V., *Steganography: A Cryptography Layer,* 1999, http://www.rit.edu/~vxr8205/crypto2/cryptopaper.html.

Rowland, C.H., Covert Channels in the TCP/IP Protocol Suite, available at http://www.firstmonday.dk/issues/issue2_5/rowland/#dep2, 1996.

Chapter 5

Watermarking

In the traditional manufacture of paper, wet fiber is subjected to high pressure to expel the moisture. If the press' mold has a slight pattern, this pattern leaves an imprint, a *watermark*, in the paper, best viewed under transmitted light. Now the old word "watermark" has been borrowed by high technology. *Digital watermarks* are imperceptible or barely perceptible transformations of digital data; often the digital data set is a digital multimedia object. While digital images are most often mentioned in the same breath as digital watermarking, we note that watermarks can be applied to other forms of digital data, for example, videos and music.

History

The watermark first made its appearance in handmade paper over 700 years ago. After the invention of the watermark, its use quickly spread through Italy and then all through Europe. It was primarily used to distinguish one paper manufacturer from another.

Watermarking is related to steganography, but is used in a different context and in a different mindset. Both watermarking and steganography are used to hide information or move information in a cover medium, but after this they begin to differ.

Steganography:

- Is not robust or has limited robustness
- Tries to hide the fact that there is hidden information

Watermarking:

- Is designed to be robust
- While not always visible, is designed to carry hidden information

With the explosion of digital art and media available, it is no surprise that digital watermarking has gained a great deal of attention since about 1995. At that time only 13 publications about digital watermarking existed; that number jumped to 103 three years later.

Classification of Watermarks

Fragile

The fragile watermark is one of the watermarking methods for authentication that has a low robustness toward modifications where even small changes of the content will destroy embedded information, showing that there has been an attempt of attack. A good example is medial records.

A fragile watermark is supposed to break. Think of it as a digital version of the foil put under the cap of a medicine bottle. It is pretty hard to get by that without it looking like it has been tampered with. Watermarks are a digital version of this idea.

Robust

A robust watermark is almost exactly the opposite of a fragile watermark. A robust watermark can be either visible or invisible, depending on purpose. Robust watermarks are very difficult to remove or damage. Following are some things to which a robust watermark can be resistant:

- *Robustness to cropping:* The watermark is embedded in so many places throughout the image that removing part of it will not remove the watermark.
- *Robustness to scaling and rotation:* This gets a bit more complicated, and without getting into the math, the simplest way to put it is the watermark algorithm has scale and rotation parameters built in that allow it to apply these "variances" when examining a watermark. These calibrated variances allow the watermark to

withstand a measure of scaling and rotation without making them unrecognizable to the algorithm.

■ *Robustness to translations:* When an image is translated, an effect called zero padding is introduced, which consists of appending zeros to a signal. This zero padding occurs, for example, when an image is scanned in from a hard-copy photo. Generally, this type of condition can be overcome by the watermarking algorithm because it is able to look for the watermark in the right place on the image and reconstruct the watermark with only about 1/3 of the watermark block.

■ *Robustness to compression:* When compression takes place, the compression regularly happens on specific frequencies of the image (typically low frequencies). With this knowledge the watermark can be embedded in higher frequencies, thus maintaining its integrity when the lower frequencies are stripped away during compression, causing a reduction in size and quality such as during JPEG compression.

■ *Robustness to other attacks:* Namely, a StirMark attack, which simulates the distortions an image would go through if it were scanned, printed, and photocopied:

1. *Unobtrusive:* While a watermark is supposed to be visible, it should be so in a manner that does not interfere with what is being protected.

2. *Robust:* The watermark should be difficult or impossible to remove, and should be immune to:

   a. *Common signal processing:* Analog-to-digital and digital-to-analog conversion, resampling, and changes to contrast, color, etc.

   b. *Common geometric distortions:* Rotation, cropping, scaling, etc.

   c. *Subterfuge attacks:* Combining multiple data sets to destroy a watermark.

3. *Universal:* The watermarking algorithm should apply to all media, image, audio, and video, which also adds assistance when watermarking multimedia.

4. *Unambiguous:* Retrieval of a watermark should identify the owner without question.

Types of Watermarks

■ *Visible:* A visible watermark is very robust because, while it is not part of the foundation image, the watermark's presence is clearly

Figure 5.1

noticeable and often very difficult to remove. An easy example of a visible watermark is a television identification logo, which is usually in the lower right- or left-hand corner of the screen. The watermark can either be solid or semitransparent, and removing it from a recording would require significant cropping, which would be instantly noticeable. For those of you who have any experience with Adobe Photoshop or another pixel-editing program, you instantly know the difficulty you would have removing the watermark in the image above without it being noticed (Figure 5.1).

■ *Invisible:* An invisible watermark's purpose is to identify ownership or verify the integrity of an image or piece of information. An invisible watermark is imperceptible, but can be extracted via computational methods. Sometimes you will see the term *data hiding*; this refers to an invisible watermark that actually contains information either about the watermark itself or the image or data in which it is embedded. Usually, when extracting an invisible watermark, a password is required; this password is called a *watermark key*. It is important to note the difference between a watermark key and an encryption key. A watermark key simply affects the watermark; an encryption key is the seed that affects the whole of the information to be encrypted. As described in the previous section about fragile watermarks, the invisible watermark is meant to be hidden, although it does not always have to be fragile. In the case of identifying ownership of a piece of information, an invisible, robust watermark would be preferable.

Reasons for Invisible Watermarking

Proof of Ownership

One major application of digital watermarking is to convey ownership. By saying that, we are also saying that there is someone who may try to take the material and misuse it by removing the ownership information. Proof of ownership information may take two forms. First, the watermark may identify the owner of the material, or second, it may identify the recipient to whom the material was given. Adding to that, these watermarks may be visible or invisible. All four possibilities make sense in the proof-of-ownership concept and all have been used in real systems.

Consider the first form of proof of ownership, watermarking the owner, and some of its benefits. A visible watermark can act as advertising by creating an unbreakable link between the image and the creator. This unbreakable link can also restrict the use of the image because no matter where it is used, everyone knows who created it, discouraging misuse. An invisible watermark could be used in a much more subtle way; it could be used as a "tag" that allows you to search the Web for your image to see if it is being misused.

Captioning is another way to watermark the owner, although this method does not necessarily act as a deterrent. Captioning embeds the watermark in the material together with associated information, for example, name, author, date, point of contact, etc. This information is usually useful to everyone. This type of watermarking is particularly good for auditing and verification. For example, a song with an inaudible watermark could be monitored to determine how many times the song is played on the radio and that it matches up with the contract the radio station signed. It could also be used to ensure that a radio or television advertisement is run the appropriate number of times.

With the explosion of DVDs in the marketplace, the movie industry has taken a strong interest in watermarking its product to prevent unauthorized copying. Tags in the watermark combined with a hardware-enabled player could allow a DVD to carry instructions to "copy never" or "copy once," allowing a user to make a backup but not unlimited copies of the DVD.

Another way is to watermark the recipient to whom the material was given or sold. This type of watermarking has raised a lot of invasion-of-privacy issues, but in reality the invasion of privacy would only come about if the recipient does not follow the agreement of the received material, meaning it should not be widely redistributed.

Secure Distribution

Using a watermark for secure distribution can provide a good deal of flexibility to the owner and distributors of the product. For example, using a watermark for secure distribution could ensure that digital contents arrive at the consumer without changes en route; it could ensure that the distributor gets paid, that the consumer's payment mechanism and privacy is protected, and that the distributor retains control of further distribution and use of the content.

Specific Watermarking Technologies

Visible Image

A visible image watermark embeds a clearly visible mark onto a gray or color photographic image. Using a watermark in this way identifies the ownership of materials and reminds viewers of their limited copying rights.

Reversible Visible

Reversible visible watermarking is a form of visible image watermarking developed at the IBM Tokyo Research Laboratory. Reversible visible watermarking is used for online content distribution. The image is marked with a reversible visible watermark before distribution, and the watermarked image content serves as a "preview" that users may view or download for free. The watermark can be removed to recreate the unmarked image by using a "vaccine" program that is available for an additional fee.

Fragile Image

Fragile image watermarking is used to determine if an image has been altered since it was watermarked. IBM is working on several techniques for exploiting this. This method of "image authentication" could be used to detect alterations or replacements in image libraries or to create a "secure" digital camera.

One of the techniques IBM is working with is used to detect the presence of tampering in an image. A robust watermark is embedded into the image simply to identify that the image is authenticated, and then another layer of fragile watermark is embedded on top; this watermark is designed to be extremely sensitive to the alteration of the image. The first layer tells the user to check the second layer; the second layer acts as an "alarm" if the image has been tampered with.

Another technique uses error diffusion to preserve the color content of an image as it undergoes watermarking. This can be important if the images are to be used in a color-critical application. This technique also retains a partial watermark; if the watermarked image is cropped, the extraction process can determine whether the remaining portion has otherwise been altered.

Both techniques require an image-specific authentication key to extract the watermark, making it more difficult for a malicious party to detect or estimate the watermark in a watermarked image. Both techniques will display the extracted watermark as an image for visual authentication, and both permit automatic authentication. Both can also localize any changes that have taken place in an altered image.

Robust Image

IBM is also investigating multiple techniques for robust image watermarking that would help identify the owner or recipient of a watermarked image. We will briefly discuss two such techniques.

1. The first technique uses a suite of technologies called DataHiding™, and was developed at the IBM Lab to allow users to embed invisible digital data into the digital content. The target media range from still image to video, and to audio data. This suite of technologies is very flexible when it comes to data payload and level of robustness; also, the data can be automatically extracted and detected without human observation or interaction.

   In still image and video DataHiding, the data to be embedded is converted to a binary bitstream and embedded into the image by altering the luminance level of the pixels following a set of predefined rules.

2. The second variation is based on a technique that modulates the brightness of the image pixels with a random noise field to embed the watermark. The color of the pixels is not altered in the watermarking, so that image color is preserved. When a watermark is extracted from an image, the watermark will be displayed even if it has been damaged by processing applied to the watermarked image. A visual inspection will quickly verify the resemblance of the inserted and extracted watermarks. In limited experiments, this technique has produced watermarks that survive printing, rescanning, reduction, and JPEG compression.

Both techniques described here require an image-specific watermark key to extract the watermark from the watermarked image. This makes it more difficult for a malicious party to detect or estimate the watermark. Both techniques insert the watermark data many times; this redundancy permits the watermark extraction to work more reliably. Neither technique requires that an unmarked image is present in order to extract a watermark.

Requirements of a Robust Digital Watermark

In order for a digital watermark to be considered up to specifications, it must meet four criteria: (1) it must appear to be invisible, (2) it must have a small probability of false detection, (3) it must be able to be embedded with a degree of flexibility, and (4) it must be difficult, if not impossible, to remove. We will consider each one of these requirements in turn.

- *Unobtrusive:* Should be invisible or if it is visible, should not interfere with what is being protected.
- *Robust:* The watermark must be difficult, or impossible, to remove.

- *Common signal processing:* The watermark should be retrievable if signal processing is applied. Signal processing includes digital-to-analog, analog-to-digital, resampling, and other signal enhancements.
- *Common geometric distortions:* Watermarks used in images and video should not be affected by scaling, rotation, cropping, or format translation.
- *Subterfuge attacks:* The watermark should be robust against the technique of combining several copies of the same data set for the purpose of destroying the watermark.

The following list expands on the previous list a little differently:

- *Imperceptibility:* The watermark should be indistinguishable from the original signal.
- *Information capacity:* The payload bit rate must be compatible with the limits imposed by the system.
- *Robustness:* The watermark must be recoverable, even after filtering, cropping, or the addition of noise to the signal.
- *Low complexity:* Needed primarily for use with real-time applications.
- *Survive multiple encode–decode generations.*
- *Tamper resistant or tamper evident:* It should be possible to recognize when a watermark has been modified.
- *Difficult to create or extract watermark without proper credentials.*

Suitable Methods for Watermarking

Patchwork

The patchwork algorithm allows for the detection of a single, specific bit in an image. Patchwork will embed in a host image a specific statistic, a small watermark that tells whether a larger watermark is embedded within an image. In short, patchwork is an indicator that tells a program that the rest of the watermark is present. While this method by itself works quite well, there have been a number of performance improvements made to the patchwork process, including treating patches at several points rather than just one, and using visibility masks to avoid putting patches where they would be easily noticed.

Patchwork is robust in its resistance to cropping and tone scale corrections. Patchwork is not robust against translation, rotation, or scaling. Because patchwork is nearly invisible, its robustness and low data rate is very suitable for digital watermarking.

Spread Spectrum

The spread-spectrum technique for encoding information can work just as well in watermarking as it does in steganography. Spread spectrum takes the information to be hidden; embeds it within the noise of the image, video, or sound file; and then inserts the modified noise back into the cover. This technique is very robust, difficult to detect, and has a good payload capability.

Orthogonal Projection

Orthogonal projection is particularly suited for digital watermarking. Its method for hiding is rather ingenious. Essentially, the image is manipulated in such a way that the hidden information is stored in the most important parts of the data and is less likely to be damaged or destroyed by compression or normal manipulation.

Because this method of encoding uses the meat of the image to its benefit, orthogonal projection is resistant to attacks such as lossy compression, photo manipulation programs, and programs such as StirMark and Unzign.

Watermarks and Compression

The practical application of watermarks in today's digital world will revolve largely around music and video. With MP3s and DVDs becoming the standard, watermarks will be used to ensure copyrights are enforced. Because most modern media uses compression in one form or another, it is important to know how watermarking and compression interact.

Cleartext PCM

Cleartext marking works by embedding a watermark into the original signal during decompression to output. For example, if you were burning a selection of MP3s to a normal, uncompressed CD format the watermark would embed itself during the decompression/writing process. Cleartext watermarks are designed to survive a variety of processes, which makes them suitable for identification. However, retrieving a cleartext watermark is very complicated and usually involves a proprietary mechanism (hardware or software) of some sort. Because of this the decoding mechanism can be reverse engineered and the watermark removed or disabled.

Bitstream Watermarking (Semantic Nonaltering)

Bitstream-marking algorithms manipulate a compressed digital bitstream without changing the basic structure of the audio or video stream. Bitstream marking uses a low-complexity algorithm and can be used to carry transaction information. This means the watermark signal is unrelated to the media signal. However, these watermarks cannot survive digital-to-analog conversion, and are generally not very robust against attacks. They are particularly susceptible to collusion attacks. This type of mark can easily be extracted by clients, and is appropriate for gaining access to content. Bitstream watermarking is an example of a security measure intended primarily to "keep honest users honest."

Bitstream Marking Integrated with a Compression Algorithm (Semantic Altering)

Integrating the watermarking algorithm with a compression algorithm avoids creating a conflict between watermarking and compression algorithms. This method creates improvements in hiding data imperceptibly in content and can lead to improvements in the perceptual compression algorithm. It also reduces the complexity of this type of watermarking. Integrated marking algorithms do alter the semantics of the audio or video bitstream, increasing the resistance to collusion attacks.

Attacks

Before we consider the types of attacks that can be used against watermarks, we will classify them so you will see how each attack tries to accomplish its objective.

Classification of Attacks

Various attacks are utilized to check the robustness of the watermarking techniques. The watermark should be detectable even in the case of severe degradation of the image due to the attack. The various attacks can be put into four main groups.

1. *Simple attack:* The simple attack does not try to separate the watermark; it mainly tries to disable or destroy the watermark while it is still part of the image. Examples of simple attacks are compression, cropping, and digital-to-analog or analog-to-digital conversions.
2. *Detection-disabling attack:* The detection-disabling attack tries to break the connection between the watermark and the image; this includes adjusting pixels or breaking the picture into several pieces.
3. *Ambiguity attack:* The ambiguity attack removes the credibility of the watermark, usually by the insertion of another watermark.
4. *Removal attack:* The removal attack tries to remove the watermark from the image. Noise filtering and resampling are examples of this kind of attack. These attacks attempt to analyze the watermarked data, estimate the watermark, and separate the mark from the data, ultimately discarding the watermark. Such attacks include collusion and denoising.

Types of Attacks

- *Collusion attack:* By looking at a number of different objects with the same watermark, one can find, isolate, and remove the watermark by comparing the copies.
- *Jitter attack:* The jitter attack works the same in watermarking as it does steganography. Its purpose is to upset the placement of the bits that identify the watermark by applying "jitter" to the image. How robust the watermark is depends on how much jitter it can take; in the case of a fragile watermark, just cropping one row of pixels from the perimeter of the image will change it significantly enough to destroy the watermark. But then again, a fragile watermark is not supposed to be able to endure a jitter attack.
- A robust watermark may fare a little better depending on the type of jitter introduced into the image. It comes back to the delicate balance between maintaining the visual appeal or integrity of the image while trying to disable the watermark.
- *StirMark:* The StirMark attack applies small distortions that are designed to simulate the printing or scanning process. If you have ever scanned in a hard-copy photograph, you know that subtle distortions are introduced no matter how careful you are. The placement of the picture on the scanning bed, the conversion

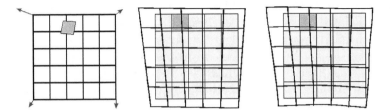

Figure 5.2

process from tangible to digital — all of these shifts can put a watermark to the test. StirMark does all of these automatically and adds multiple distortions on top of one another. Some of the distortions StirMark uses are JPEG, scaling, rotation and cropping, rotation, scale and cropping, shearing, flip, change of aspect ration, row and column removal, and random bending, just to name a few. This attack is particularly effective because some watermarks are more resistant to one type of modification as opposed to another, but usually are not immune to all of them at the same time (Figure 5.2).

■ *Anti soft bot:* A benefit of watermarking in the realm of the Internet is the ability to use software robots, sometimes called soft bots or spiders, to search through Web pages for watermarked images. If the soft bot finds a watermarked image, it can use the information to determine if there is a copyright violation.

■ *Attacks on echo hiding:* Echo hiding is a signal-processing technique that places information imperceptivity into an audio data stream in the form of closely spaced echoes. These echoes place digital tags into the sound file with very little sound degradation. Echo hiding is also very resistant to jitter attacks, so a removal attack is the usual method for getting rid of the watermark. In echo hiding, most echo delays are between 0.5 and 3 milliseconds; in anything above 3 milliseconds, the echo becomes noticeable. To remove the echo, the attacker uses the same method as detecting it, only with some modifications. The process of echo detection is called cepstrum analysis, and the attacker would use this process with an opposite signal to damage the watermark.

■ *Additive noise:* This attack is fairly straightforward; it simply involves adding additional, imperceptible noise to the image to hinder or stop the watermark detection process. Because each pixel in the image has a tolerance for the amount of noise that can be introduced and still remain invisible, the additive noise attack uses that tolerance value to introduce the maximum amount of uncertainty that the decoder will have to deal with.

- *Linear filtering:* Linear filtering is used when an attacker wants to eliminate a watermark or destroy any information that identifies the author or owner. This attack is carried out by removing an estimate of the watermark from the marked image, restoring the original image. Sometimes this "estimate" watermark can cause damage to the data, depending on the complexity of the information the watermark is embedded into.

- *Resampling:* Resampling combines analysis and interpretation of a data file to change it by a certain factor. What that essentially means is a program will look at an image file, for example, interpret the pixels it "sees," and assign a new approximate value to them. It will also look at the surrounding pixels for more information about the image. Then it takes these new values, based on estimations, and puts everything back together, creating a new image. The tolerances set in the beginning determine how much variance happens during the resampling process.

  Having said that, it is easy to see how this can be an effective attack for rendering an invisible watermark useless. By taking a new estimation of the original, the watermark will cease to exist.

- *Cropping:* Often a watermark is embedded in a linear fashion, meaning that the pixels that comprise the watermark follow a pattern that cropping can do significant damage to, depending on the extent of cropping. If the watermark is embedded in a pseudorandom fashion, the watermark may be more resilient to cropping, but removing pixels is still removing pixels, and it will weaken the energy of the watermark.

- *The mosaic attack:* This attack relies on the fact that a watermark cannot be embedded into a small image. This attack disables the watermark by splitting the image into small pieces and then putting them back together. This creates the illusion that the image is really one picture, not a series of small ones. But as far as the detection method is concerned, it does not see one image; it sees a number of them, and none of them contain the watermark it is looking for (Figure 5.3).

Fingerprinting

Fingerprinting is a special application of watermarking that applies specifically to information that is embedded about the creator of the work or the recipient. Fingerprinting has the characteristics of one object that distinguish it from another, very similar object. The real-world use of digital fingerprinting enables owners to trace authorized

 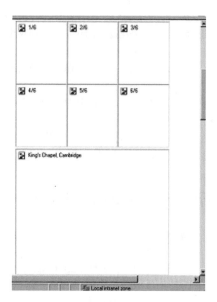

Figure 5.3

users distributing their material illegally. It can also be used as a means of high-speed searching.

Fingerprinting Examples

- Human
- Fired bullet
- Serial number
- Coded particles of explosives
- Maps

Digital Fingerprints

- Prefixes of e-mail addresses
- PGP public keys
- Digital audio or video
- Documents

Terminology

- *Mark*: A portion of an object with a set of several possible states
- *Fingerprint*: A collection of marks

- *Distributor:* An authorized provider of fingerprinted objects
- *Authorized user:* An individual who is authorized to gain access to a fingerprinted object
- *Attacker:* Someone who gains unauthorized access to fingerprinted objects
- *Traitor:* An authorized user who distributes fingerprinted objects illegally
- *Labeling:* Where embedded data contains information of interest, such as a unique identifier

Fingerprinting Classification

- Object-based classification
  - Physical fingerprinting is where an object has characteristics that can be used to differentiate it from something else.
  - Digital fingerprinting is a fingerprint in a form that a computer can process.
- Detection-sensitivity-based classification
  - Perfect fingerprinting is any alteration that makes the fingerprint unrecognizable.
  - Statistical fingerprinting allows an examiner to compare fingerprint alterations to confidently determine that a compromised user has been identified.
  - Threshold fingerprinting allows for a certain number of illegal uses, but when that number is reached or passed, it identifies it as an illegal copy.
- Fingerprinting-method-based classification
  - *Recognition:* Human fingerprints.
  - *Deletion:* A portion of the original object is deleted.
  - *Addition:* A new portion is added to the original object.
  - *Modification:* A deliberate change to some portion of the object is made for identification.
- Fingerprint-based classification
  - *Discrete:* The fingerprint has a finite hash value.
- *Continuous:* The fingerprint has an infinite value, a human fingerprint.

Summary: Diversity of Digital Watermarks

Watermarks can be used in a variety of diverse and flexible ways, as the previous sections have outlined. A watermark's diversity does not end simply with perceptibility, however. Robustness is another dimension of watermarking as well as the techniques used to embed a watermark. In this spectrum of diversity a watermark carries data and the forms of that data.

Bibliography

Bender, W., Gruhl, D., Morimoto, N., and Lu, A., *Techniques for Data Hiding,* IBM Systems Journal, 35, 3 and 4, 1996.

Braudaway, G.W., *Protecting Publicly Available Images with an Invisible Image Watermark,* IBM Watson Research Center.

Cox, I.J., Kilian, J., Leighton, T., and Shamoon, T., *A Secure Robust Watermark for Multimedia,* University of Cambridge, U.K., 1996.

Eggers, J.J., Su, J.K., and Girod, B., *Asymmetric Watermarking Schemes,* University of Erlangen-Nuremberg, 2000.

Gruhl, D. and Bender, W., *Information Hiding to Foil the Casual Counterfeiter,* Information Hiding Workshop, 1998.

Hartung, F. and Girod, B., *Watermarking of Compressed and Uncompressed Video,* University of Erlangen-Nuremberg, 1998.

Hernandez, J.R. and Perez-Gonzalez, F., *Throwing More Light on Image Watermarks,* Universidad di Vigo.

Herrigel, A., Ruandiadh, J.O., Peterson, H., Pereira, S., and Pun, T., *Secure Copyright Protection Techniques for Digital Images,* University of Geneva.

Judge, J.C., *Steganography: Past, Present, and Future,* SANS, 2001.

Katzenbeisser, S. and Petitcolas, F.A.P. (Eds.), *Information Hiding: Techniques for Steganography and Watermarking,* Artech House, Boston, 2000.

Marvel, L.M., Boncelet, C.G., Jr., and Retter, C.T., "Reliable Blind Information Hiding for Images," International Workshop on Information Hiding, April 1998.

Mintzer, F., Lotspiech, J., and Morimoto, N., "Safeguarding Digital Library Contents and Users," *D-Lib Magazine,* December 1997.

Swanson, M.D., Kobayashi, M., and Tewfik, A.H., "Multimedia Data-Embedding and Watermarking Technologies," *IEEE,* 86, 6, June 1998.

Wu, M., *Silent Messages and Invisible Pictures,* Electrical Engineering Dept., Princeton University, 2000.

Chapter 6

Steganography Tools

Anahtar

Anahtar is a program that prepares a key disk for copy protection. The program generates a key disk that is readable by your program only and embeds a password onto a 3.5-inch diskette. This protection key can be detected only by the person creating the disk. When the program is launched, and the password is not made available when called for, the program will end. More information about this program can be found at http://anahtar.artshost.com.

BackYard

BackYard is a steganographic file system program that can completely hide and protect files, folders, and drives by making them completely inaccessible, i.e., hidden from the Windows® operating system, write protected, or from any other protection scheme you specify. Different protection profiles can be created with different files and directories, and can be activated with a single hotkey. BackYard also has a built-in search capability to find and protect your files. Features include:

- Make any file or directory invisible
- Write protect any file or directory
- Make any file or directories attributes unchangeable
- Make any file or directories attributes impossible to delete or read

- Make any directory deny a file or sub-folder creation
- Protect all files with a specific extension or an entire drive

More information about this program can be found at www.talya-soft.com/backyard.shtml.

Blindside

Blindside is a steganography application that allows you to conceal a file, or set of files, within a single digital image. The resulting image appears identical to the human eye, but can typically contain around 50 kb of secret data. The concealed files can also be password protected. Blindside operates by creating slight color inflections in an image which, although invisible to the human eye, can provide a great deal of space in which to store information. Blindside calculates the color differentials between pixels and will modify the image only where it can be sure no one will notice. A proprietary cryptographic algorithm can also be used to scramble the data with a secret pass phrase. More information about this program can be found at www.blindside.co.uk.

BMP Secrets

BMP Secrets is another steganography program that allows you to store any information in a bitmap file. One big advantage of BMP Secrets is that it has a very large hiding capacity. Some features include:

- The program uses an original steganography method developed by Parallel Worlds that allows you to replace up to 65 percent of the true-color BMP file with your data. You can convert the result image only to lossless format; lossy formats will destroy information inside. If you try to make any changes to the result image, information will also be lost.
- You can choose hiding rate. The higher the hiding rate, the lower the quality. However, if you use the highest rate it is difficult to find any differences.
- A built-in to encoding compressor that allows the storage of much more text files than binary.
- You can hide not only in whole image, but also in part. You can choose a rectangle on the picture where data will be stored. Sometimes you can store two different files in two different squares of one image. It also increases the security level.

- You can set an automatic quality option. The program will search for the best quality when the whole file can be stored.
- Hiding spreads data all over the image when you provide a password. To withdraw an encoded file and to decode it is very difficult, because nobody except you knows the data-spreading order period.
- You can view results of your hiding and compare the original with the result.
- If the whole file cannot be placed in one picture, the file can be split. When you unhide this file, you can bring parts together into one file, allowing you to hide one big file in several images. It also increases the security level, as far as one needs all parts to extract hidden file.

More information about this program can be found at www.pworlds. com/products/secrets.html.

bProtected® 2000

bProtected® is steganographic file system that provides security at the lowest operating system level. Using an advanced file-based protection scheme, it can secure everything by preventing unauthorized access to resources and information stored in the computer.

There are four protection levels:

1. Completely hiding files and folders
2. Blocking any access to the files and folders
3. Allowing just read-only access to files and folders
4. Monitoring file and folder data usage

More information about this program can be found at www.clasys. com.

BuryBury

BuryBury is another steganographic file system that lets you manage files and keep them out of sight. All files are securely encrypted, renamed, and buried on your hard drive. No one can determine the true nature of your files by title, length, or extension name. BuryBury uses a Windows Explorer® interface with password protection so that it appears that all your "special" files are visible when actually they are buried. All data is strongly encrypted using the TwoFish algorithm.

Camera/Shy

Camera/Shy is a browser-based steganography application from Hacktivismo, a special operations group sponsored by another famous hacker group, the Cult of the Dead Cow. It is the only steganographic tool that automatically scans for and delivers decrypted content straight from the Web. It is a stand-alone, Internet Explorer-based browser that leaves no trace on the user's system and has enhanced security. Camera/Shy was designed and developed for democracy activists who are restricted by firewalls.

Camera/Shy is very easy to use and was in fact designed for the nontechnical user. The features listed here show that it is both user friendly and effective:

- User friendly and Web browser based
- Automatic invisible cache and history clearing built in
- Automatically scans Web pages for stegged and encrypted GIF files
- Web page encoding into GIF functionality
- Parsing of hidden content functionality
- All content scanned and parsed down from the local cache
- Automatic Rijndael encryption of all steganographic content
- Least-significant byte pixel insertion steganography
- Relative links that would be broken made into static links in Web site encrypting process
- High and moderate security browsing settings, including:
  - Optionally killing all active scripting, including DHTML behaviors
  - Optionally killing all Java and ActiveX applications
  - Optionally disabling client pull in cases where you want to ensure the content comes from the server or local cache you are browsing
  - Stand-alone executable file, no installer
  - GIF to and from BMP, and JPEG to and from BMP utilities built in for easy GIF content selection (Figure 6.1).

About Hacktivismo

Hacktivismo is a group of international hackers, human rights workers, artists, and others who seek to further the goals of human rights through technology. Operating under the aegis of the Cult of the Dead Cow (cDc), Hacktivismo is committed to developing technologies in support of the highest standards of human rights. More information is available at http://hacktivismo.com.

Figure 6.1

About the Cult of the Dead Cow

The Cult of the Dead Cow (cDc) is the most influential hacking group in the world. The group is further distinguished by publishing the longest running E-zine on the Internet and stretching the limits of the First Amendment. The cDc is known for fighting anyone, individual or government, that aspires to limit free speech. More information is available at http://cultdeadcow.com.

Camouflage

Camouflage is an interesting program in that it allows you to hide files by first scrambling them and then attaching them to a file of your choice. This "camouflaged" file then looks and behaves like a normal file. It can be stored, used, or e-mailed without drawing attention.

With Camouflage you can create a picture file that looks and behaves exactly like any other picture file but contains hidden encrypted files, or you can hide a file inside a Word document that would not attract attention if discovered.

Camouflage allows for additional security by providing a password function for the file. This password will be required when extracting the files within. You can even camouflage files within camouflaged files.

One point to note is that the hidden file can be detected by examining the raw file data. Examining the data in this way will reveal that a hidden file has been added after the normal carrier data, even though the data will appear as gibberish because the data is encrypted. While not the most secure form of steganography, its ability to use inconspicuous files makes it an effective tool. More information about this program can be found at www.camouflagesoftware.co.uk.

Cloak

Cloak is a program used to encrypt and hide files within bitmap pictures. Files hidden with Cloak are not only undetectable, but irretrievable as well. Cloak uses advanced technology to protect files, including:

- Cloak-128/Blowfish/Mercury encryption algorithms
- Custom security certificates
- Optimized compression
- Password protection of files

You can secure any file type with Cloak, including .exe files. Bitmap pictures containing hidden files are fully functional and are identical to the original bitmap picture. Cloak also includes a very powerful image converter to convert images to 24- or 32-bit bitmaps. More information about this program can be found at http://insight-concepts.com.

Contraband (Hell Edition)

This Windows-based program embeds and extracts any type of file into 24-bit bitmaps. Contraband is a steganography tool first, but it does have a weak encryption algorithm. The Uncontra program will break the encryption (Figure 6.2).

Courier

A free program by Kelce C. Wilson, Courier hides text messages in bitmap files (Figure 6.3). More information about this program can be found at http://pages.prodigy.net/robyn.wilson/.

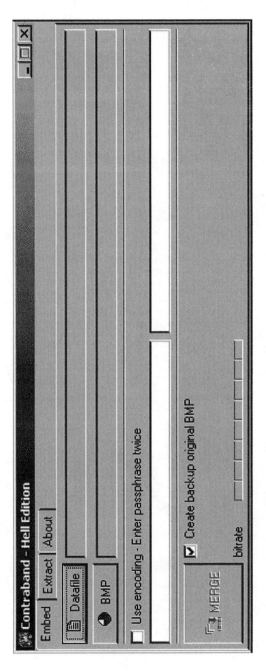

Figure 6.2

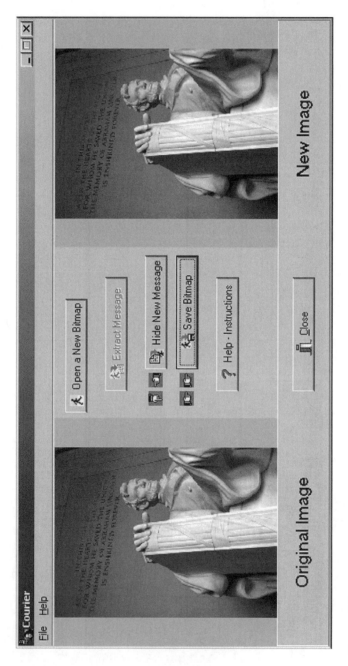

Figure 6.3

Crypto 123

Crypto 123 is primarily designed as an encryption program, but it also allows you to embed encrypted messages into another file. Features include:

- Encrypt and decrypt text files and files within files.
- Encryption can be password protected.
- Encrypted text messages can be embedded into any other file (i.e., bitmap picture).

More information about this program can be found at www. kellysoftware.com.

Dark Files

Dark Files is a Windows platform file-administration program that has a steganographic file system setting. The program provides three levels of protection: hidden, read-only, and full control.

Dark Files can work with network folders and removable media on all platforms. The file system protection works independently of the program, and the multiple user interface allows you to use Dark Files without any change in settings on multi-user systems. If the computer is configured for use by multiple users, you can define the list of protected folders separately for each user.

Data Stash

Data Stash allows you to hide sensitive data files within other files. Select a file to use as a receptacle, and then add the data files you would like to hide. The receptacle file remains fully functional. Features include:

- Hide files within other files.
- Drag and drop.
- Receptacle file remains functional.
- Password protection using Blowfish encryption.

Digital Picture Envelope

Digital Picture Envelope uses a new steganographic technique called BPCS-Steganography. This technique was invented by Eiji Kawaguchi of Kyushu Institute of Technology. It can embed information in bitmap or GIF cover data. Embedding is made on the bit planes of the image. The most important feature of this steganography is that its embedding capacity is very large.

Disk Hide

Disk Hide is a small program that "hides" the definitive drives on a computer. By making alterations in the registry, the program makes it impossible for Windows to load a drive, and blocks access to records without the need for the drive to be physically detached. Disk Hide creates a "blocked" drive that is ignored by almost all programs that run on Windows.

Dound

This free steganography program allows users to encode and decode messages with their choice of keyword. The program was inspired by the movie *Along Came a Spider* (Figure 6.4). More information about this program can be found at http://evidence-eliminators.co.uk/dound. htm.

DPT 32

DPT 32 is another encryption program that has steganographic capability. DPT makes it possible to hide any encrypted data: text, executable, .dll, etc., in a picture file (Figure 6.5).

DriveCrypt

DriveCrypt allows you to hide sensitive information in .wav files. Password allows authorized users to access secret information; anyone else will find only harmless music files. More information about this program can be found at www.securstar.com.

Drive Hider

Drive Hider allows you to be selective about which drives you allow users to see. It does not matter if they are actual physical drives on

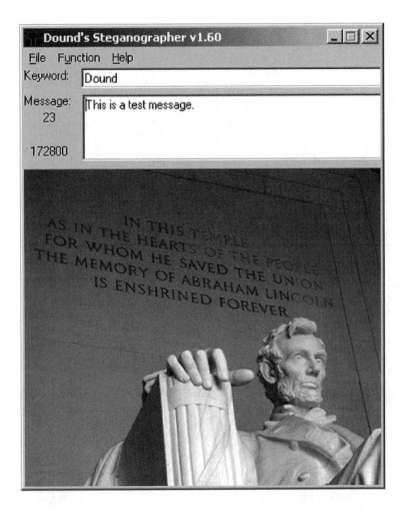

Figure 6.4

the local machine or logical drives. Any of these drives can be hidden from selected users.

Easy File & Folder Protector

Easy File & Folder Protector protects files and folders on local media of Windows platforms at the kernel level. You can restrict access to certain files and folders, or hide them securely from viewing and searching, and the program does not modify any media while protecting your files (Figure 6.6). More information about this program can be found at www.softstack.com.

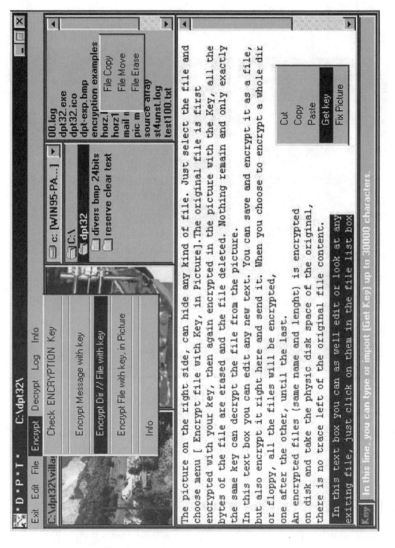

Figure 6.5

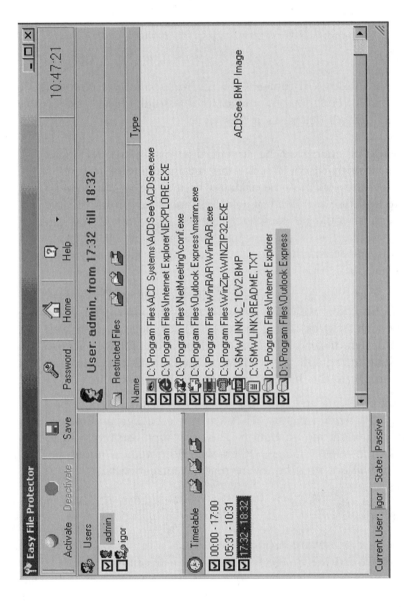

Figure 6.6

EasyMemo

EasyMemo uses steganography and cryptography as a safe storage area for data. The data can be stored in coded .jrm, .bmp, or .png files locally, on an intranet, or the Internet.

EmptyPic

This program hides GIF images within Web pages by changing the picture from a recognizable image into a solid color. The creator, Robert Wallingford, describes it this way:

> When I first conceived the system, this was a black rectangle. Then I saw that I could make this rectangle any of 16 million colors. Now you must be asking why anyone would want to make a picture that is all one color. If this were an irreversible process, it would be completely useless. However, if you can easily restore the original picture, there are many useful applications on the Internet. Some of these applications may even be legal.

> Most of us have at least one graphic file that we don't want everyone to see. We can now use mask.com to make it a single color such as black. Then, in the HTML language used in Web page design, instead of using a background color we can use this "masked" graphic. The HTML language will even automatically replicate this hidden image to fill the desired area.

> On the receiving end, selected users know that the background contains a hidden picture. They can "save background image" with their right mouse button. They can then use fixx.com to restore the original image. Others who do not know about this system will not even be aware that the image exists.

EncryptPic

EncryptPic is a shareware program that hides a file in a 24-bit bitmap. You can password the image using the Cast algorithm (Figure 6.7).

EzStego

EzStego is a free program by Romana Machado that can hide an encrypted text file in a GIF format image file. It is a stand-alone Java

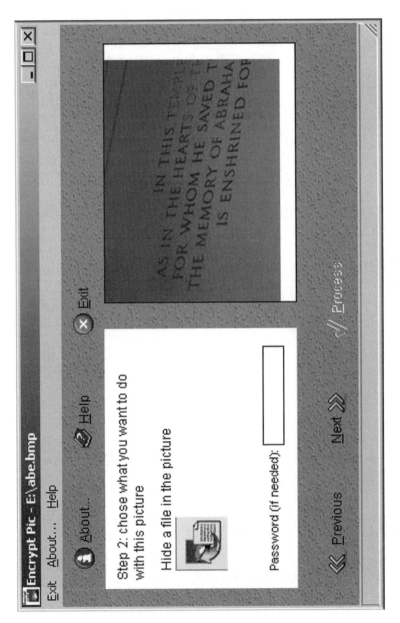

Figure 6.7

application. More information about this program can be found at www.stego.com.

F5

F5 uses a Java runtime environment and a new steganographic algorithm that allows it to embed files into true-color BMP, GIF, or JPEG images.

FFEncode

FFEncode is a DOS program that hides a file in a text file by using a "Morse code" of NULL characters. Simply type FFENCODE or FFDE-CODE at the DOS prompt for the command line parameters.

File Protector

File Protector is a utility to protect files and folders. File Protector can hide files in a variety of ways by making them:

- Undeletable
- Unrenameable
- Unreadable
- Unmodifiable
- Unexecutable
- Invisible

More information about this program can be found at www.mikko-tech.com.

Folder Guard™

Folder Guard™ makes files and folders invisible or read-only, controls access to system files, restricts access to the Control Panel, and prevents unauthorized use of a stand-alone or networked computer. Folder Guard makes files or folders invisible to all applications, no matter what file system your drive is formatted with (Figure 6.8). More information about this program can be found at www.winability.com/folderguard.

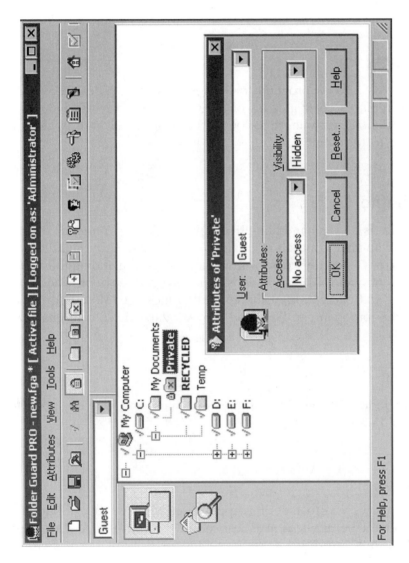

Figure 6.8

GhostHost

GhostHost is a freeware program that uses steganography in a special way. It attaches the file at the end of the file host instead of hiding a file inside an image or a sound. This program does not work well with text files.

Gif-It-Up

Gif-It-Up is a stego program for Windows 95 that hides data in GIF files. It replaces color indexes of the GIF color table with indexes of "color friends," meaning a color in the same table and as close as possible to the original.

Gifshuffle

Gifshuffle is a command-line-driven, public-domain program by Matthew Kwan that conceals messages in GIF images by shuffling the color map. Gifshuffle works with all GIF images, including those with transparency and GIF animations. The program also provides compression and encryption of the concealed message. More information about this program can be found at www.darkside.com.au/gifshuffle.

GZSteg

GZSteg hides data in GZip compressed files, and was compiled for DOS by Preston Wilson.

Hide It

Hide-it allows you to hide any application window and its button in the taskbar; the application is also removed from the Alt-Tab chain, so it will not disturb your task switching, as if it just is not there. To unhide it, you right-click in the small icon in the system tray area and select it. This program provides more of a covert channel than a means of steganography.

Hide4PGP

This freeware, command-line-driven program was created out of concerns that the public use of cryptography would become illegal. Hide4PGP works on everything from 8- to 24-bit bitmaps, 8- or 16-bit .wav files, and 8-bit .voc files. It works especially well on 256-color bitmaps.

Hide Drive

Hide Drive is a Windows NT/2000/XP utility that allows you to hide one or more drive letters. The drive letter will not show up in My Computer or any of the standard Windows dialog boxes. Hide Drive is not totally robust, and hidden drives can be detected by other means. Its purpose is to hide information from the casual Windows user. Some uses for Hide Drive can be to hide backup images or files so they are not accidentally deleted or to hide personal files on a computer that is used by more than one person. More information about this program can be found at www.iscreations.com.

Hide Drives

Hide Drives, plural, is another software tool that basically does the same thing as Hide Drive except that it works on all Windows platforms. When a drive is hidden in Hide Drives, it is not visible in Explorer or any other application that uses common Windows dialog boxes such as Save, Save As, and Open. Again, Hide Drives can be used for protecting critical files or to keep files private on a computer that is used by more than one person (Figure 6.9).

Hide Folders

Hide Folders is a steganographic file system program from FS Pro Labs. With a mouse click, all selected folders become invisible. Once enabled it is impossible to find hidden folders, access any file in it, and remove it (even when removing an upper-level folder). Features include:

- Supports NTFS, FAT32, and FAT volumes.
- Up to 64 folders may be hidden at the same time.

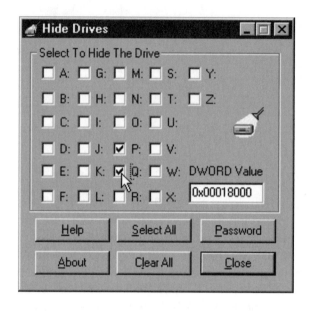

Figure 6.9

- No file system structure modifications will occur.
- Effective password protection when running or uninstalling program.
- Removing Hide Folders XP folder from the system will not uncover hidden folders.
- Files from hidden folders will not be lost even if someone tries to remove an upper-level folder.
- Cannot detect the program with Windows Task Manager.

More information about this program can be found at www.fspro.net.

Hide In Picture

Hide In Picture is a freeware steganography program by Davi Figueiredo that allows you to "hide" any kind of file inside a standard bitmap. The program also has a password protection function.

Hide Me

Hide Me is a clever Windows program that hides otherwise unhideable desktop icons behind your desktop's wallpaper. While it is possible to remove most of the desktop icons within Windows, there are a few (such as My Computer) that are a little more permanent. Hide Me creates a small window that sits directly on top of those icons, grabs the wallpaper from underneath the icons, and paints itself with that portion of the wallpaper. The icons seem to disappear. Clicking on its taskbar icon toggles the icons back and forth (Figure 6.10).

Hide-Seek v.5

Formerly a command-line-driven program, Hide-Seek Version 5 comes with a rudimentary interface. Using GIF files, the program can embed and encrypt information within a cover image. For this program to be the most useful, grayscale images are recommended.

Info Stego

Info Stego is a steganography and watermarking tool that allows you to protect your private information, secret communications, and legal copyright using information watermark and data encryption technology. Info Stego can hide your important information and copyright mark inside another file, which can be picture, sound, video, etc. As with any steganography or watermarking program, other people cannot notice the change of the file with eyes and ears (Figure 6.11).

InPlainView

This program allows you to hide any type of file inside a 24-bit bitmap and recover it. InPlainView supports long file names, and has drag-and-drop capability and password protection. More information about this program can be found at www.9-Yards.com

InThePicture

InThePicture allows you to embed files and messages into .bmp files. Some features include:

- Multiple unique keys that are useful for encrypting data intended for multiple recipients of the same file
- A drag-and-drop interface

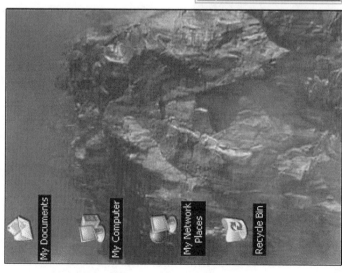

Figure 6.10

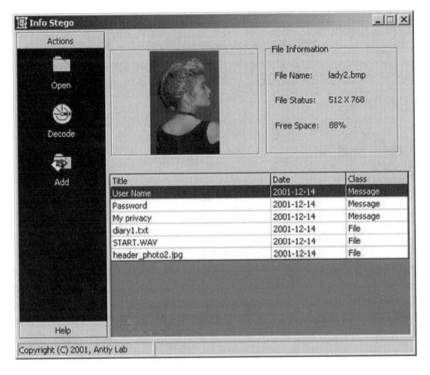

Figure 6.11

- Can generate its own cover images in BMP format in the event few BMP files are available
- Supports 16, 256, and 16 million color BMPs

More information about this program can be found at www.intar.com.

Invisible Files 2000 Pro

Invisible Files 2000 Pro (IF2000 Pro) is a program for Windows 95/98/ME that allows hiding of any file or folder on the local hard drives of personal computers. The files are not physically deleted but they are invisible (even in Windows safe mode and DOS session). File systems FAT16 and FAT32 are supported. IF2000 Pro also supports long file names, and has a function where you can safely wipe the critical information you want deleted.

Invisible Secrets

Invisible Secrets 2002 encrypts your data and files for safekeeping or for secure transfer, and can hide them in pictures, sound files, or Web pages. More information about this program can be found at www.neo-bytesolutions.com.

JP Hide and Seek

JP Hide and Seek is actually two DOS-based programs, jphide and jpseek, that hide files inside JPEG images. One very unique feature of these programs compared with other steganography programs is these are designed to have a very low insertion rate, usually less than 5 percent, which maintains the quality of the image. A newer program is available, JPHSWin, which combines both programs with a Windows GUI.

Some tools have characteristics that are unique among stego-tools. In Versions 4.1 and 5.0 of Hide and Seek, the color palettes have a very unique characteristic that have yet to appear anywhere else. All color palette entries are divisible by 4 for all bit values.

Jsteg Shell

Jsteg Shell reads almost any lossless picture format and saves the output file as a JPEG. An important note from the authors is this program does not read JPEGs; it only exports the final product in JPEG format. This has several benefits. First, saving a stego-image as a JPEG makes the file that much more unnoticeable because it is the *de facto* standard for the Internet and newsgroups. Second, steganographic information is more difficult to detect with the naked eye in a JPEG image than it is in other formats.

KPK File

KPK File provides security for your sensitive files by encrypting and hiding them. It has a steganography option, allowing the user to bury an encrypted file within another still-working file, such as a Microsoft Word document or a bitmap image. KPK File can also create secret folders that are impossible to access without the proper password.

Magic Folders

Magic Folders is a shareware program that makes a folder/directory and all files in that folder completely invisible to anyone without the correct password. Once made invisible, the folders cannot be viewed, modified, deleted, or run. The program also allows multiple accounts, so many different invisible folders can exist on one machine, and these folders can be shared as needed.

MASKER

MASKER is a steganography and encryption program that supports several high-performance coding algorithms, including Cast-256, Blow-fish-256, Rijndael-256, and Twofish-256. The cover image can be an audio file, a program, or a video file. Once the hidden information is embedded, the file is still fully functional. Additionally, files can be compressed for network transmission.

MergeStreams

This utility allows you to merge Word and Excel streams. This technique can be used to hide an Excel document inside a Word document or vice versa. The program does not implement cryptography and by itself is not very secure.

MP3 Stego

MP3Stego, or MP3Steno as it is also called, will hide information in MP3 files during the compression process. Data is first compressed, encrypted, and then data is hidden in the MP3 bitstream. Although MP3Stego has been written with steganographic applications in mind, it could also be used as a watermarking system for MP3s. An opponent could uncompress the bitstream and recompress it, deleting the hidden information, but at the expense of severe quality loss.

NICETEXT

NICETEXT uses the technique of linguistic steganography in a very inventive way. The goal of NICETEXT is to provide a program that can transform ciphertext (encrypted text) into text that looks like natural language while still providing a cover for the original ciphertext. An added benefit of this type of program is that it can be applied to many different languages. The software works by sampling certain aspects of writing by style or by using context-free-grammars (CFG).

NICETEXT relies on large code dictionaries consisting of words categorized by type. A style source selects sequences of types independent of the ciphertext. NICETEXT transforms ciphertext into sentences by selecting words with the matching codes for the proper type categories in the dictionary table. The style source defines case sensitivity, punctuation, and white space independent of the input ciphertext. The reverse process simply parses individual words from the generated text and uses codes from the dictionary table to recreate the ciphertext.

NookMe

NookMe is a shareware utility that gives you the ability to manipulate Windows in a variety of ways. Features include:

- Make windows disappear from desktop and taskbar.
- Choose how a window minimizes or disappears.
- Automatically hide any window on startup.
- Lock hidden window using a password to prevent unhiding.

OutGuess

OutGuess is a Linux program that preserves statistics based on frequency counts. This means that as a result no known statistical test is able to detect the steganographic content within the JPEG cover. OutGuess determines the maximum message size that can be hidden while still maintaining the statistics based on frequency counts. OutGuess tries to find a sequence of bits that minimizes the number of changes that have to be made in the data.

PC FileSafe

PC FileSafe allows you to lock up individual files or folders and set a password so that only selected users can gain access. The best feature

Ulysses S Grant

Figure 6.12

is that files that are locked cannot be seen and the information cannot be obtained.

Phototile

Phototile is a shareware program that creates a large mosaic-like image made of many smaller photos. Use your own digital photos or combine with the supplied collections (Figure 6.12). More information about this program can be found at http://www.prismaticsoftware.com.

Picture Messenger

Picture Messenger enables the user to conceal a binary or text file in a Windows BMP. The carrier file should be a 24-bit uncompressed .bmp file. The message document can be any other file with a size limit of 10 kb. It also encrypts the message before concealing it into an image file, so no one else with a copy of Picture Messenger would see the message.

Point Lock PRO

Point Lock PRO allows you to set protection for your computer system and data. It guards your system against data leaks to snoopers and unauthorized users both on the Internet and on your local area networks. Point Lock PRO also prevents unintentional deletions and modifications to your protected files caused by operational mistakes or malicious intent by unauthorized users.

PRETTY GOOD ENVELOPE

PRETTY GOOD ENVELOPE is a program suite for hiding a (binary) message in a larger binary file, and retrieving such a hidden message. The algorithm simply appends the message to the binary envelope file, and then puts the appended 4-byte pointer to the start of the message. To retrieve the message, the last 4 bytes of the file are read, the file pointer is set to that value, and the file is read from that point, excluding the last 4 pointer bytes.

PRETTY GOOD ENVELOPE is implemented so that it physically alters the envelope file as found on disk, rather than reading it and rewriting it. Full DOS file specification is supported, up to a maximum of 36 characters. When retrieving a message, you have complete control over the naming of the output file.

Any character in the command tail will cause this file to be output to the screen, provided it is either in the current directory or a directory in the DOS path specification. No options or file specs are supported in the command line except for this .doc file. PGE Version 1.0 was written by an author using the alias Roche'Crypt.

PrivateInfo

PrivateInfo is a utility that helps you protect your private information from other people. It makes your information, files, and folders invisible from the operating system, even DOS. PrivateInfo also allows you delete your information without the possibility to restore.

Protector

Protector is a data hiding program that allows you to:

- Create user accounts for users using your computer.
- Allow access to your computer only for certain users.
- Define user rights to any folder or file for each user.
- Really hide hidden files for defined users.

Protector will enforce the specified user rights for the file system on your computer and protect system registry from changes that could damage Protector itself or change system policy settings.

RightClickHide

RightClickHide can completely hide and protect your files, folders, and drives by making them fully inaccessible and invisible. It is easy to use and integrates itself into the right-click menu of Explorer. With no limits on protected files, it is available to use with any Explorer-type program. RightClickHide protection is user friendly and secure. Files and folders are protected in a way that they do not appear at all on your computer.

While navigating the protected items is easy through the Control Center of RightClickHide, protection can be turned on and off with a single click. It can run silently in total stealth mode and will not be visible to others using your computer.

Sam's Big Play Maker

Sam's Big Play Maker is a Win32 program that converts arbitrary text to an amusing play script (Figure 6.13).

SandMark

SandMark is a system for embedding a watermark in a Java program. It modifies the application source code to make it build a structure at

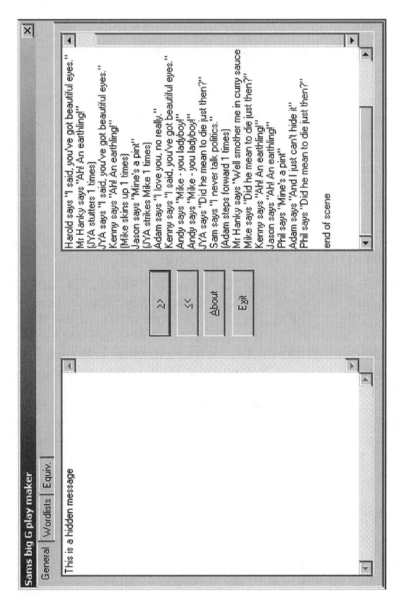

Figure 6.13

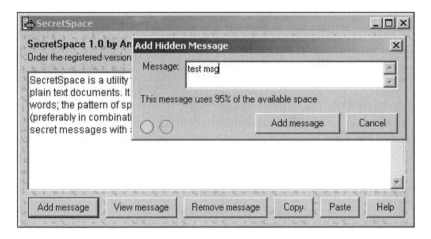

Figure 6.14

execution time that encodes a watermark. The watermark is recognized by dumping and analyzing the Java heap.

The ultimate goal of SandMark is to produce application watermarks that an adversary can remove only through careful analysis, but not through automated means.

Scramdisk

Scramdisk is a program that allows the creation and use of virtual encrypted drives. Basically, you create a container file with a specific password on an existing hard drive. This container can then be mounted by the Scramdisk software, which creates a new drive letter to represent the drive. The virtual drive can then be accessed only with the correct pass phrase. Without the correct pass phrase the files on the virtual drive are totally inaccessible.

Secret Space

Secret Space is a utility that allows you to conceal short messages invisibly within plain text documents. It does this by inserting superfluous spaces between words; the pattern of spaces stores the message data (Figure 6.14).

SecurDesk!

SecurDesk! is made up of four separate main modules: desktop, task manager, file manager, and administration manager. Together they offer a variety of options that may be used alone or in conjunction with other security measures to control access to sensitive files and settings, replace Explorer.exe, verify who is using your machine, hide confusing and irrelevant items from selected users, ease training tasks, track system usage, etc.

SecurDesk! allows you to construct your own desktops with multiple levels of password access. It contains its own powerful file manager with built-in security, a task manager/Start bar replacement, and the tools you need to configure an environment suited to your unique needs and security concerns.

Snow

Snow (steganographic nature of white space) is a program written by Matthew Kwan. Snow is a rather unique steganographic tool in that it relies on white space, line spaces, and tabs that appear as blanks in text viewers. The program works by adding spaces and tabs to the end of lines in ASCII text files. Within these spaces and tabs lay the pieces that make up the secret message. The program size is very small. At 61 kb, Snow fits on a floppy with room to spare for files and secret message files.

Spam Mimic

Spam Mimic is a process that the people over at spammimic.com have developed to encode and decode e-mail messages to be disguised as spam. Considering the amount of spam that is sent around the Internet, and also considering that most people either filter it at the mail server or just delete it, it is really an ingenious idea. This makes security through obscurity a reality. For example, if a terrorist group wants to coordinate some type of action with its followers in the United States, using an anonymous e-mail application or a hacked server, the message could be sent to a huge mailing list, as spam is. The people who are expecting the mail could simply decode the spam-encoded message. Why not just use PGP or some other encryption software? The answer is that if you are afraid of being monitored, encryption leaves an obvious trail and is easily detected. If you are monitoring traffic, a simple spam message could easily slip through undetected as it has the form of plain, ordinary text.

StealthDisk

StealthDisk is a revolutionary, patent-pending security system enabling you to completely hide any kind of data on your computer. Any type of files, folders, and complete applications may be hidden. Any type of file search or software audit will not be able to reveal the existence of data hidden with StealthDisk. Data is completely hidden in all computer operational modes, including safe mode, MS-DOS, and boot from floppy drive. Accessing your hidden files requires a hotkey combination and your password.

Steghide

Steghide is a steganography program that embeds a secret message in a cover file by replacing some of the least significant bits of the cover file with bits of the secret message. After that, the secret message is imperceptible and can only be extracted with the correct pass phrase. Steghide is able to embed data in .jpeg, .bmp, .wav, and .au files.

Steganosaurus

Steganosaurus is a plain text steganography utility that encodes a binary file as gibberish text, based on either a spelling dictionary or words taken from a text document.

StegoTif

StegoTif will hide a message into a given TIFF 24-bpp picture. This is done by changing the value of the least significant bits for each RGB (Red Green Blue) channel to the value retrieved from the message.

StegoWav

StegoWav hides a message in a given RIFF (8/16 bits) PCM .wav file. If the message is shorter than required to cover the full image, random noise will be added. It is better to compress the message with a lossless compressor such as .zip (or pkzip), so that it will appear more "random" and will not generate patterns on the coded image.

S-Tools

S-Tools (Steganography Tools) is a program written by Andy Brown. It is perhaps the most widely recognized steganography tool available today. BMP, GIF, and WAV files can be used as the cover files that conceal the secret messages. It is easy to use, with simple dragging and dropping of the files. S-Tools will hide the secret message within the cover file via random available bits. These available bits are determined through the use of a pseudorandom number generator. This nonlinear insertion makes the presence and extraction of secret messages more difficult.

S-Tools Tutorial

Figure 6.15 shows the S-Tools main working windows. The dark gray background area is used for dropping the image or sound files into. This area is for insertion and extraction of the secret message. The lighter gray "Actions" window shows the status of tasks taking place.

After opening S-Tools (S-Tools.exe) and Windows Explorer, drag Cover File.gif into the main working area of S-Tools. Figure 6.16 shows this cover file GIF in the main working area. Note the text that appears in the bottom right corner. S-Tools analyzes the GIF and outputs the approximate number of bytes available for storage. For this example, there are 44,984 bytes available for hiding data (Figure 6.16).

To hide the secret file, drag secret file.doc into the S-Tools working area and over the cover file as shown in Figure 6.17.

At this point S-Tools prompts for a pass phrase. The pass phrase is used in generating the pseudorandom number that is used to insert the bits into the cover file. S-Tools gives a choice between IDEA, DES, TripleDES, and MDC encryption algorithms. Figure 6.18 shows the pass phrase box.

The pass phrase and encryption algorithm must be remembered in order to extract the secret file. If IDEA was used during the hiding process and DES is selected during the extraction process, the secret file will not be extracted. Enter a pass phrase and select IDEA as the encryption algorithm.

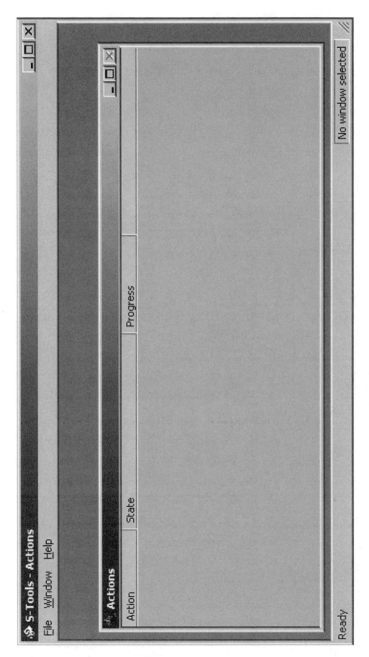

Figure 6.15

Figure 6.16

Figure 6.17

Figure 6.18

To have S-Tools process the GIF file, a dialog box prompts for choices to be made. The choices affect how the cover file will be processed during the insertion of the secret file. The picture options box is shown in Figure 6.19.

Accept the defaults and now S-Tools will begin the process of hiding the secret file within the cover file. The ACTION sub-window will display the status of the processes (Figure 6.20).

When S-Tools finishes inserting the data, the output image will display with the marker "hidden data" at the top. This GIF is the product of inserting the secret file into the cover file. In order to save this new file, right click and select Save As. The new output file can be named anything you like at that point (Figure 6.21).

Similar to the method used in the stego file system, S-Tools will spread the file bits out throughout the free space on the floppy. This is undetectable in the normal Windows viewer, but the file is there.

S-Tools Version 3 has the ability to embed information in unused tracks of a floppy disk. While this program is not widely available on the Internet these days, it is still possible to find it and you may encounter this particular function.

How It Is Done

S-Tools will allow you to hide files in the unused space on floppy disks. To understand what is meant by unused space, look at the way DOS organizes the files on a disk. Every floppy disk, when formatted, is divided into sectors. Each sector on a disk can hold 512 bytes of information. On a 1.44-Mb disk, there are $1440 \times 1024/512 = 2880$ sectors. When you write a file to the disk, DOS computes how many sectors it will need to hold the file and writes this information into the file allocation table (FAT).

Figure 6.19

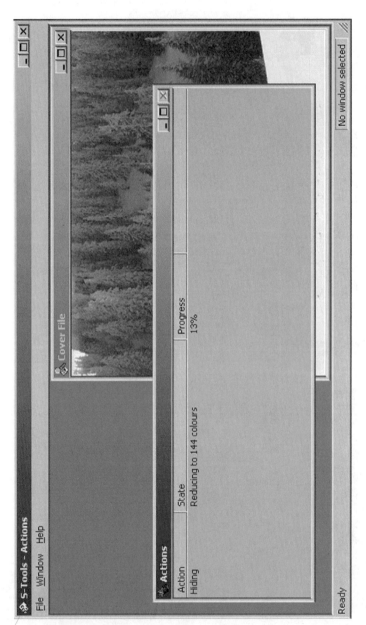

Figure 6.20

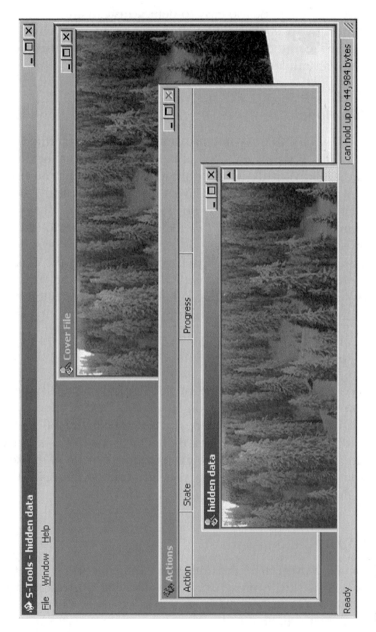

Figure 6.21

S-Tools' FDD module will look at the FAT to decide which disk sectors have not been used, and will allow you to hide information on them. S-Tools will not hide information in consecutive sectors on disk because this would be too easy to detect. Instead it uses a random number generator to choose which free sectors to use. S-Tools will add additional security by allowing you to fill all other unused sectors on the disk with random data.

Using This Module

There are a few tips that you might want to be aware of when using the FDD module. If you want to be able to plausibly deny having any concealed data on your disks, it would make sense to fill the unused space on all your newly formatted disks with random data. This way any concealed data will appear to be "lost in the noise."

One point to remember with this feature of S-Tools: Do not write any ordinary files to the disk after you have concealed information on it. Depending on the amount of space you have left on the disk, it is very likely that DOS will overwrite your hidden information. This point can also work in your favor because there may be a situation where you want the hidden information destroyed.

Analyze Disk

This option displays a usage map of the floppy and tells you how much information you can hide on it. S-Tools will work with any capacity of disk that DOS can use, up to a maximum of 1.44 Mb. Sectors marked in red are the ones that S-Tools cannot use because files are already stored there. The status bar at the bottom of the screen will tell you how much information you can hide on the disk (Figure 6.22 through Figure 6.24).

Fill Free Space

This option allows you to fill the unused sectors on a disk with random data. This will mask the presence of any file that you want to hide on the disk. S-Tools automatically asks you whether you want to fill the free space after hiding a file.

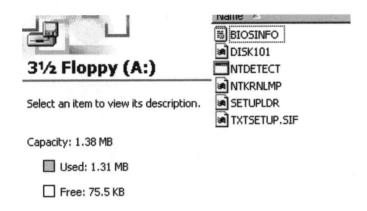

Figure 6.22

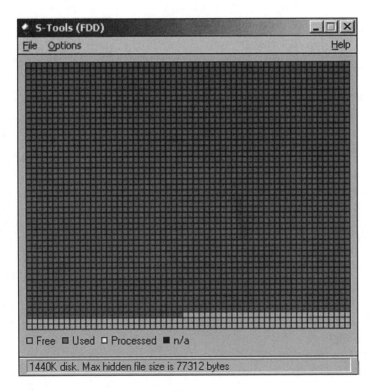

Figure 6.23

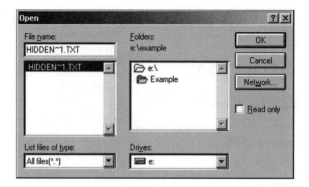

Figure 6.24

A Word of Warning

If you fill the free space on a disk *after* hiding a file, you will lose that file. After hiding, S-Tools will forget about its presence until you use the reveal operation. If at any time you decide you want to stop the process, hit the Escape key.

Hide File

This is the option that you use when you want to hide a file on disk. If you are not sure whether the disk has enough free space to hold the hidden file, then you can use the Analyze Disk option to find out.

First you are asked to choose the file that you want to hide. If you have asked to be prompted for encryption options, you will be asked whether the file should be encrypted before hiding. Using encryption is recommended even if the file is already encrypted because the pass phrase that you enter is also used to seed the random number generator that is used to choose the sectors that will hold the hidden file. Again, if you want cancel the operation press the Escape key (Figure 6.25 through Figure 6.27).

Reveal File

This is the option that you should use to reveal a file that has been hidden on a disk. Simply insert the disk into the disk drive and select this option. If encryption was selected as an option when the file was embedded, then you must supply the correct pass phrase in order to reveal it. If everything works as planned, S-Tools will look at the disk

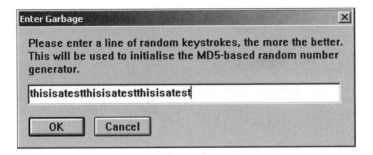

Figure 6.25

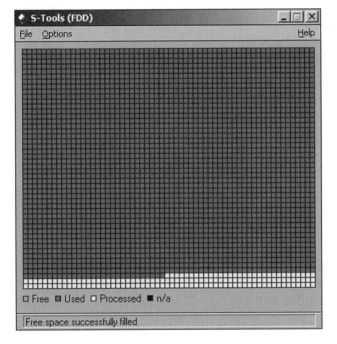

Figure 6.26

and decide whether a file is hidden on it. If there is a hidden file, the program will tell you the size of the file and give you the option of viewing it or saving it.

Conclusion

S-Tools is roughly 589 kb in size, small enough to fit on a floppy. As is the case with many steganography programs, S-Tools leaves little in

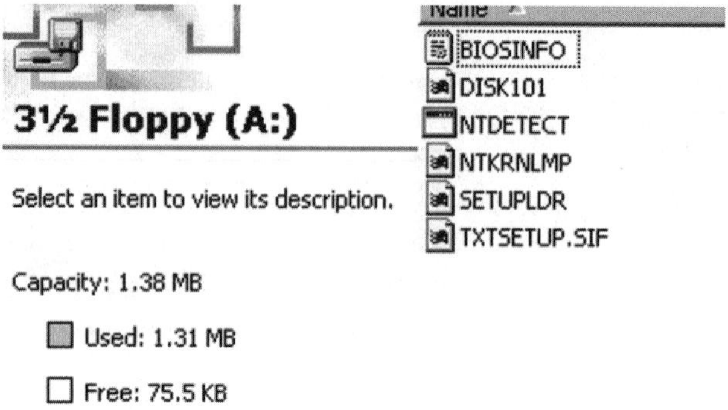

3½ Floppy (A:)

Select an item to view its description.

Capacity: 1.38 MB

☐ Used: 1.31 MB

☐ Free: 75.5 KB

Name

🔲 BIOSINFO
🔳 DISK101
🔲 NTDETECT
🔳 NTKRNLMP
🔳 SETUPLDR
🔳 TXTSETUP.SIF

Figure 6.27

the way of a footprint. However, there is a known signature of S-Tools. S-Tools reduces the number of colors in the cover file to a minimum of 32. In doing so, grayscale images are affected. There exists a more detailed explanation of this, but it goes beyond the goal here. In sum, a true grayscale image may no longer be a true grayscale image due to the change in the palette indexes. So this palette signature becomes a way to distinguish one image from another with a secret file embedded. However, because of the strong encryption that can be set, the secret data still has a very good chance of remaining a secret.

SysCop

Syscop processes a grayscale image; it reduces the total number of colors to only the colors needed in the final stego-image. The result of using this tool on a GIF image that has a color index of 256 will be that the index will now show only those few colors used by Syscop.

Texto

Texto, which was written by Kevin Maher, is a text steganography program that transforms uuencoded or PGP ASCII data into English sentences. Texto text files look like something between mad libs and bad poetry (although they do sometimes contain deep cosmic truths) and should be close enough to normal English to get past simple-minded mail scanners (Figure 6.28).

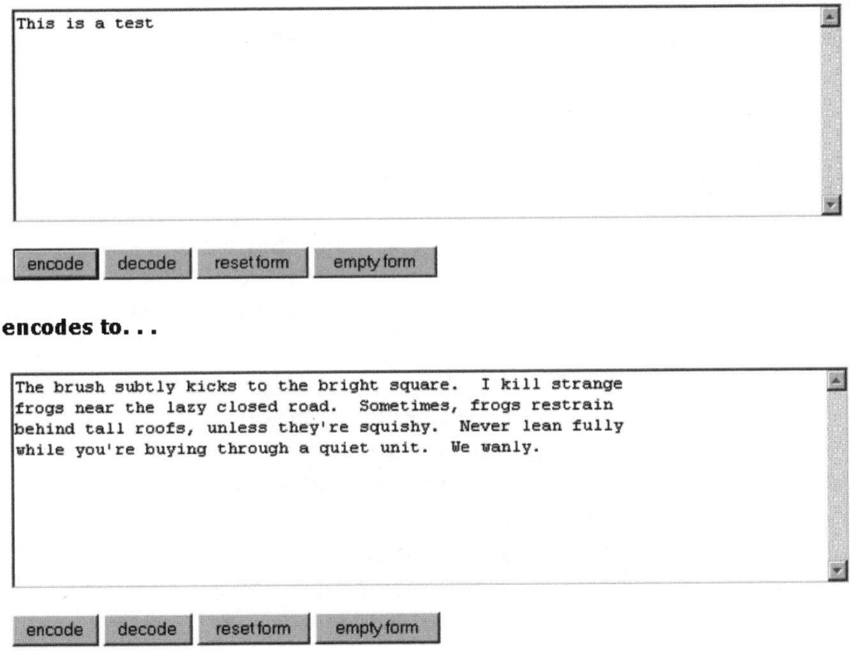

```
┌─────────────────────────────────────────────────────────────────────┬─┐
│This is a test                                                       │▲│
│                                                                     ├─┤
│                                                                     │ │
│                                                                     │ │
│                                                                     │ │
│                                                                     │ │
│                                                                     ├─┤
│                                                                     │▼│
└─────────────────────────────────────────────────────────────────────┴─┘
```

| encode | decode | reset form | empty form |

encodes to. . .

```
┌─────────────────────────────────────────────────────────────────────┬─┐
│The brush subtly kicks to the bright square.  I kill strange         │▲│
│frogs near the lazy closed road.  Sometimes, frogs restrain          ├─┤
│behind tall roofs, unless they're squishy.  Never lean fully         │ │
│while you're buying through a quiet unit.  We wanly.                  │ │
│                                                                     │ │
│                                                                     │ │
│                                                                     ├─┤
│                                                                     │▼│
└─────────────────────────────────────────────────────────────────────┴─┘
```

| encode | decode | reset form | empty form |

Figure 6.28

WbStego4

WbStego4 is a steganography tool for Windows 95/98/NT/2000. It hides data inside bitmap images, ASCII and ANSI text files, HTML files, and Adobe Acrobat (PDF) files. For the encoding and decoding process, two user-friendly interfaces are provided. WbStego4 is designed for transmitting data safely online and also for adding copyright information.

White Noise Storm

White Noise Storm is a very effective steganography application for DOS. White Noise Storm includes an encryption routine to randomize the bits within an image. The software uses the least-significant bit approach and applies this method to IBM Paintbrush (PCX) files. The main disadvantage of applying White Noise Storm's encryption method to steganography is the loss of many bits that can be used to hold information. Relatively large files must be used to hold the same amount of information that other methods provide with much smaller cover images.

The Latest and Greatest: Hydan

Rakan El-Khalil, a Columbia University computer science Masters candidate, has recently released an application that lets users hide a secret message in virtually any executable computer program without changing the program's size or affecting its operation. The tool is called Hydan, which means "the act of hiding something."

El-Khalil's research focused on redundancies in the Intel x86 instruction set — places where at least two different instructions are effectively the same. Each choice between two redundant options can represent a single bit of data. A computer instruction to add the number 50 to another value, for example, can be replaced with an instruction to subtract the number −50 instead. Mathematically, the instructions are the same. In choosing between the two, a stego program can get one bit of covert storage out of each addition or subtraction operation in the executable, without changing the way the application runs or adding a single byte to its size.

This technology could also be used to attach a digital signature to an application or to embed an executable with a virtual watermark.

Chapter 7

Products and Companies

Alpha-Tech Ltd. (W)

Alpha-Tech is a research and development company specializing in digital image, multimedia, and video processing. Alpha-Tech has a number of watermarking technologies that can be applied to almost any type of digital media.

EIKONAmark

EIKONAmark is software for casting "invisible" watermarks on digital images and detecting these watermarks. EIKONAmark can be used for copyright protection and "ownership" recognition of digital images. A copyright owner can cast its ID number as an "invisible" watermark on any digital image. Later, he can examine whether a given image, which is suspected of being illegally copied, contains his own ID number, and use it as legal proof.

AudioMark

AudioMark is a software package designed for casting "inaudible" watermarks on digital audio and detecting them in case of controversial ownership. The primary usage of AudioMark is copyright protection and supply of ownership evidence for digital audio. A copyright owner uses a unique key to create an "inaudible" watermark on its audio files. Later, he or she can examine whether a given audio file, which

Note: (W) Watermarking
    (S) Steganography

is suspected of being illegally copied, contains his or her own watermark, and use it as legal proof.

VideoMark

VideoMark is software for casting and detecting invisible watermarks on digital video for copyright protection. Watermarks correspond to specific ID numbers called watermark keys. Each copyright owner of digital video uses a private key to cast an invisible watermark. This watermark can be detected later by using the VideoMark and the correct watermark key without resorting to the original product.

VolMark

VolMark is a powerful and flexible software package for embedding and detecting three-dimensional watermarks on digital, grayscale, and three-dimensional images. It can be used for copyright protection of three-dimensional images. A copyright owner can embed a unique, personal key number as a three-dimensional watermark in digital three-dimensional images. The results of three-dimensional watermark detection can be used either for security applications or as legal proof.

More information can be found at www.alphatecltd.com.

AlpVision (W)

AlpVision, located in Switzerland, provides digital multimedia data watermarking, multimedia data security, and image and video processing services. AlpVision's products of interest are SignIt!, LabelIt!, and digital video watermarking services.

SignIt!

SignIt! is digital image processing software that can hide and retrieve an invisible registration number from a signed image. The registration number is hidden everywhere in the image and cannot be seen by the naked eye. It is impossible to remove the embedded registration number without altering the image in a visible way.

In combination with the Inter Deposit Digital Number (IDDN), SignIt! helps you protect the copyright of your images. The IDDN number uniquely identifies your original work and provides legally valid copyright protection of your image. By linking your image to the IDDN number, SignIt! allows you to track your images after distributing them and to identify illegal copies. This unique combination of IDDN's worldwide trusted registration procedure and AlpVision's digital watermarking technology currently provides one of the most effective and efficient copyright protection systems.

LabelIt!

The LabelIt! application enables you to hide a string of 20 characters in any scanned picture, meaning that whatever the electronic image is used for (word, publishing, e-mail, Web site, etc.) it will always be possible to know the original material from which it was scanned.

Digital Video Watermarking

AlpVision video watermarking technology enables you to hide data in digital or analog video. This data can be used for tracking, fingerprinting, copyright infringement detection, or any other application that requires some hidden data.

PhotoCheck

PhotoCheck creates a protected image with an identification number. This number is embedded in the image and it is also written in cleartext below the picture. This new image can then be saved and used, for instance, with plastic card printers. More generally, any printer can use this image to output secured identification documents.

The second operation is to check the validity of an identification document that has been created by PhotoCheck. Once the document has been placed on the scanner, the operator just presses the "check document" button. This automatically starts the scanning process and document analysis. After a few seconds, a window pops up and informs the user whether the document has been counterfeited or is valid.

More information can be found at www.alpvision.com.

BlueSpike (W)

BlueSpike specializes in digital watermarking technologies in order to "preserve creators' custody of their works and yet maintain the balance of interests between creators, distributors, and consumers as defined under copyright law." BlueSpike's signature product is a watermarking program called Giovanni.

Giovanni Digital Watermarking Suite

Giovanni is a genuine digital watermarking system. This patented system provides a means for creators of multimedia content to protect their copyrights on computer networks or other digital media such as compact discs, as well as track content that is electronically distributed. Giovanni can be simply differentiated from other digital watermark systems by its use of "keys" in the watermark process. These keys are separate from the actual encoding and decoding process. Essentially, Giovanni allows copyright holders to create encoded messages, break them up into single bits, and plant them in random locations in a signal. Those bits are locatable only by the same key that was used to place the bits of the watermark payload.

Principles behind Giovanni Digital Watermarks

All digital samples have a built-in allowance for error, because they are only approximations of an analog signal. Even if the digital data is badly damaged, it is still often recognizable when played or viewed.

Giovanni binds a digital signature to a recorded music digital signal in a manner that ensures that attempts at erasure cause audible damage to the song. Secure BlueSpike watermarks can be used to tamperproof individual instances of a digital copy of any media content.

For watermarking, not just encryption, encoding and encryption are handled by the key as well. The private key is used to encode the digital watermark into the music. The public key is used to decode the digital watermark from the music without revealing the private key. The consumer can even authenticate a copy of a song with a public key, just like a purchase receipt.

Giovanni watermarks can be both a digital signature and a digital fingerprint. In a similar manner to encryption, Giovanni can use digital signatures. The process of embedding a watermark into a digital sample stream is not a digital signature calculation, as is executed in public key cryptographic systems. The information encoded by Giovanni is digitally signed, however, to certify the validity of the information when it is extracted. In so-called asymmetric or public-key cryptography, a file encoded with the "private" key of a user's key pair can only be decoded with a correlative "public" key.

Giovanni watermarks can be applied to any data consisting of digitized samples, such as digital audio, video, and still images. The watermarks can also be completely removed with an authorized key. Giovanni watermarks are also able to survive analog conversions in both audio and still images.

More information can be found at www.bluespike.com.

Compris (W) (S)

Compris provides a way of inserting a digital watermark into text using a product called TextMark.

TextMark

This method for digital watermarking of information is very difficult to remove because an attacker would also need to model the complete language correctly in a computer.

Scanning, Speech Recognition, Internet Downloading, and Intelligent Text Processing Systems

Text processing becomes increasingly simple; writing good texts remains difficult. With TextMark you have the ability to protect your intellectual property. This innovation distinguishes itself by its broad applicability to all kinds of textual documents and its tamperproof characteristic.

The problem that led to the creation of TextMark was how to embed a watermark into a text-based format. A common method changes the word distances slightly and operates with similar concepts as watermarking tools for images. Unfortunately, it is extremely simple to remove such a watermark in images and text completely. Currently existing pirate tools enable any school boy to remove such watermarks. The text, the image, or the song by itself will still remain, allowing the work to be copied and resold, or to be published unauthorized on another Web site. In such cases, chances of proving authorship are slim.

The solution was to directly integrate the digital watermark into the text using a rephrasing technique. The text rephrasing is minimal, which means only a slight change in the choice of synonyms, word order, positions of additional blanks for block justification, etc. The meaning of the text will be retained fully because the program is able to understand language. Sections that cannot be completely understood remain unchanged. The watermark can be hidden as often as possible in the text.

TextHide

TextHide was designed with one goal in mind: Create the most secure and most inconspicuous method for transmitting and storing information. To add to this, TextHide uses the best-known encryption methods and additionally the encrypted information is hidden so that it cannot be recognized as such. Everyone is able to decode something from the text, but if the text was previously encrypted, it cannot be determined that the decoded data is relevant. Because it is not obvious whether the data present is encrypted, no direct decryption attack can happen. When using obviously encrypted data, an eavesdropper will try to find the kind of encryption method to specifically crack this method.

To solve this problem, TextHide uses the best encryption method and hides the data in texts. The attacker will believe he is reading unencrypted text. Even when encrypted data is suspected, the encryption method used is still unknown. The TextHide method is also able to decode secret data from any kind of text. The decoded data will only make sense when meaningful data has been previously hidden in the text. An attacker is not able to distinguish encrypted data from meaningless data.

More information can be found at www.compris.com.

CenturionSoft (S)

CenturionSoft publishes and markets software products designed for the consumer and business markets, focusing on security, productivity, and communications utilities.

Steganos 4 Security Suite

Steganos 4 is a complete set of utilities to protect your privacy and secure important documents. It is a total security solution and one of the first to use 128-bit Advanced Encryption Standard.

Steganos 4 has a feature called "Encrypt and Hide," which employs steganography. The program conceals confidential information in sound or image files after first encrypting it. It is then possible to send sensitive data via the Internet without risk of discovery.

More information can be found at www.centurionsoft.com.

Central Research Laboratories (CRL) (W)

CRL's Audio Watermarking is a technique for embedding data codes within audio in such a way that the perceived quality of the audio is undisturbed. In a music application, it can be used for persistent identification in the following ways:

- An ID code can be added during production transaction.
- Tracking codes identifying the purchaser can be added when the music is sold or played.
- Access control codes can be added that enable a user to play or copy the music; this can also be used to prevent a user from playing or copying music.

CRL's Audio Watermarking technology has the benefits of audibility, high payload, and robustness. The robustness features include:

- Analog-to-digital and digital-to-analog conversion
- Compression (e.g., MP3, AAC)
- Radio and TV broadcast (AM, FM)

More information can be found at www.crl.co.uk.

Data Dot Technologies Ltd. (S)

Data Dot Technologies has taken the concept of the microdot and modernized it into a new and effective technology. Their mission statement is

> to supply the world's leading anti-theft identification technology solutions and encourage community support for marking property with a police traceable ID so as to reduce apathy toward the problem of theft and enhance the effectiveness of law enforcement to deter thieves.

Data dots are security encoded microdots that are the size of a grain of sand and practically invisible to the naked eye. Yet these data dots can easily be found and identified with powerful magnification by a user or the authorities. The adhesive that bonds the data dots to any surface shines under ultraviolet light. While it may be possible to remove some of the microdots, many will remain hidden and thus impossible for thieves to find and remove.

As an example, 10,000 Data Dot vehicle identification number dots are sprayed across the key component parts of a motor vehicle. This makes the parts as easily identifiable as the whole, and therefore too "hot" for thieves to handle.

More information can be found at www.mdatatech.com/australia/about_us.htm.

DataMark Technologies

DataMark Technologies provides digital watermarking technologies geared toward business-to-business and business-to-customer areas of the economy. Their technology has the same characteristics of most digital watermarks, enabling a user-invisible mark to be added to documents and multimedia files. DataMark's solution also provides robust protection against analog-to-digital and digital-to-analog conversions.

More information can be found at www.datamark-tech.com.

Digimarc ®

Digimarc has quickly become the global leader in digital watermarking technology used to authenticate, validate, and communicate information within digital and analog media.

Digimarc ImageBridge™ Watermarking

- Communicate image copyrights
- Track images as they travel the Web
- Enable image licensing and commerce opportunities
- Enhance asset management applications

Digimarc MarcSpider™ Image Tracking

Digimarc MarcSpider image tracking technology combines Digimarc's Web crawler and data feeds from Web search engines, allowing it to cover over 50 million images a month. MarcSpider is a subscription service to which you are given unlimited access to online reports about where your images are found.

Digimarc MediaBridge™

Digimarc MediaBridge technology uses an "embedder" program that adds a digital watermark to prepress digital image files. There are two ways to embed a Digimarc MediaBridge digital watermark: (1) an Adobe PhotoShop plug-in and (2) for jobs requiring many unique watermarks, the Digimarc variable embedder.

Embedding a digital watermark is easy, and there are many techniques that allow the prepress designer to get the best image quality and easy readability.

The Digimarc MediaBridge Reader software works with an ordinary Web cam or scanner. This program detects a digital watermark in a printed piece of media and then routes the user to a Web page.

Secure Documents

Secure Documents helps brand owners and document issuers defend valuable documents, products packaging, and cards against the digital counterfeiting threat with digital watermarking security features.

More information can be found at www.digimarc.com.

eWatermarking

eWatermarking provides a technique that enables everyone to easily protect digital content copyrights without having to perform complicated procedures. eWatermarking also provides a technique for authenticating digital content. The products are designed for those content holders, such as Webmasters, creators, and photographers, who want to protect their copyrights online.

SteganoSign

SteganoSign is a software program that can embed and detect digital watermarks in various types of images and audio data. SteganoSign can embed digital watermarks in popular image formats such as JPEG, BMP, PCX, TIFF, and PCT. For audio data, it supports .wav files. SteganoSign is equipped with a scanner input feature. SteganoSign can also embed a digital watermark or hide a document in a handwritten manuscript or drawing.

Variable Display Digital Watermark

Variable Display Digital Watermark is a new digital watermarking scheme to color images, which can display the mark in a visible-to-invisible state. eWatermarking proposes a digital, visible watermarking scheme to color images, which controls the color transformation between the RGB and YCbCr color systems for each pixel. In this scheme, a logo-mark is displayed in a visible-to-invisible style on the color image. The displayed mark is changeable to an invisible or half-visible state when it is requested. Then, the original image is recovered smoothly, but the watermark remains in the invisible state. Using this method, the author can show the copyright in various states and may change the displayed mark to an invisible one without losing the watermark signal that protects it against StirMark attacks.

More information can be found at www.ewatermark.com.

InterTrust

InterTrust develops and licenses intellectual property for digital rights management (DRM), digital policy management (DPM), and trusted computing. InterTrust software and hardware techniques can be implemented in a broad range of products that use DRM and trusted computing technologies, including digital media platforms and Web services, and the enterprise infrastructure.

More information can be found at www.intertrust.com.

Macrovision

Macrovision is another company that specializes in digital rights management (DRM) solutions.

SafeAudio

SafeAudio is designed to protect against piracy. The SafeAudio solution starts at the CD manufacturing site. Once implemented at the site, any customer can request the SafeAudio copy protection. SafeAudio is transparent to the consumer. It supports the widest range of playback devices and supports multi-session, PC-compatible CDs with digital rights management (DRM) extensions.

More information can be found at www.macrovision.com.

MarkAny

MarkAny's goal is to create a secure and safe digital environment that allows new ideas and technologies to be shared without worries about losing creditability and copyrights.

Document Safer

Document Safer grants authority to read, print, transfer, edit, upload, and download according to each user's security level and responsibility. The activity of each user is recorded on the server and processed to statistics.

Multimedia Contents Safer

Content Safer is watermarking technology and DRM that protects copyright as well as illegal copy and distribution of digital contents. Content Safer ensures safe transactions with the application of a secure billing system, and it reports the transaction statement of contents as it supports optimal marketing.

MarkAny Web Safer

MarkAny Web Safer prevents all the copy functions of the contents on the Web site.

MarkAny DRM

MarkAny Light-Right DRM is used for multimedia content copyright protection and incorporates a billing system to guarantee safe distribution. MarkAny Light-Right DRM solution manages Key Management Server by itself so it is able to manage the whole process from creation, distribution, and extermination of all kinds of content.

MAIM 2.0: MarkAny Image Watermarking

MAIM protects copyright information of image providers by embedding copyright information invisibly into the image. MAIM allows image providers to distribute images without any legal violations.

MAO 2.0: MarkAny Audio Watermarking

MAO is a copyright protection product that embeds copyright information into an audio file. The copyright information is inaudible and allows people to distribute their audio works while protecting against illegal copying.

MarkAny Video Watermarking: Esignia™-Video 1.5

Esignia-Video (MAVI 2.0) protects copyright of video contents by embedding watermark into the contents. The watermark is invisible and can be quickly embedded and extracted. Esignia-Video allows you to distribute your video contents on the Internet without worrying about illegal copy and distribution.

More information can be found at www.markany.com.

MediaSec Technologies

MediaSec provides products and solutions to solve problems in the fields of document security and authentication, anticounterfeiting, brand protection, and copyright protection.

MediaSignDigital™

MediaSignDigital offers a highly secure and effective solution to protect digital images and video against unauthorized alteration or manipulation. MediaSignDigital provides permanent and inseparable image and video authentication that is invisible to the naked eye. It embeds the secure hash value of the data's semantics into the image or frame in the form of a digital watermark. Authentication features include content, time, source, and sequence verification. MediaSignDigital is an emerging standard that can be used to validate the integrity of digital evidence in court.

MediaSignPrint™

MediaSignPrint offers an authentication solution based on digital watermarking that prevents forgeries of ID documents. MediaSignPrint allows ID issuers to securely embed personal information within the image on the document. The watermark is invisible to the naked eye but machine-readable and can link textual information on the document to the image in such a way that they are inseparable and can be cross-verified. MediaSec's patented MediaSignPrint technology protects valuable documents such as passports, driver licenses, access cards, checks, and credit cards.

MediaSignPrint can also be used in brand protection applications.

MTL Systems, Inc.

MTL specializes in five core technology application areas:

1. Specialized information services
2. Image and signal processing
3. Modeling and simulation
4. Sensor systems testing
5. Engineering services

Advanced Digital Watermarking (ADW) Tool

ADW is used for information hiding, file tampering detection, image tagging, digital signatures, and file access control.

More information can be found at www.mtl.com.

SealTronic Technology, Inc.

SealTronic Technology's products are based on digital watermarking, data hiding technology, and Digital Rights Managements. SealTronic provides consulting services in the field of multimedia contents security and electronic document authentication. SealTronic Technology develops technologies involving copyright protection and verification, contents security for electronic governments and companies, and authentication and tracking of forged multimedia documents.

Multimedia Content Security Products Group (RIGHTS@fer Multimedia)

The RIGHTS@fer Multimedia Product Group is designed and developed to support the download, streaming environment for distribution of multimedia content and to prevent illegal reproduction of content with user authentication and encryption. This product group is designed for secured, convenient usage of content in various environments such as the wired/wireless environment, peer-to-peer services, satellite, or IP broadcasting, etc.

- RS Media
- RS Streaming

Authentication Products Group (MagiCheck)

MagiCheck is designed to overcome the weakness of digital content, which is easy manipulation. Due to this weakness of digital content, it cannot be admitted in courts as evidence. MagiCheck solutions ensure authenticity of the digital content by applying authentication watermarks. MagiCheck can be applied to various digital imaging documents, digital camera images, photographs, and surveillance video images such as in government, public organizations, financial institutions, hospitals, etc.

- MC Document
- MC Image
- MC Video

Copyright Protection Products Group (MagicTag)

MagicTag Products Group is designed to protect rights of copyright holders. MagicTag solutions provide proof of copyright ownership of digital content such as images, video, and audio files.

- MT Image
- MT Video
- MT Audio

More information about these programs can be found at www.seal-tronic.com.

Signum Technologies

Signum Technologies is a vendor of advanced digital data protection and integrity technology. Signum's data integrity, authentication, and copyright protection software are also marketed as VeriData and SureSign. Driven by the needs of a diverse client base, Signum Technologies' responsive research and development and business teams continue to shape the future direction of the company's advanced watermarking solutions.

SureSign

The SureSign Software Development Kit (SDK) for audio, video, and still images allows application software developers to quickly integrate SureSign watermarking tools into a wide range of audio applications.

VeriData iDem

For many users of digital photography, ensuring the integrity and authenticity of digital images is a primary consideration, especially in situations where photographic evidence may be subject to judicial or ethical scrutiny. VeriData iDem software was specifically developed in conjunction with forensic scientists and crime-scene investigators to overcome the problem of digital image integrity. iDem can detect that an image has been modified and can also pinpoint the site of any localized alteration. The software provides a useful audit trail to support the chain of evidence, such as identifying who processed the image, when it was processed, and which workstation it was processed on. It can validate images created with almost all makes and models of digital cameras or scanners.

VeriData iDem is now in widespread use with law enforcement and government agencies and blue-chip corporations worldwide who need to ensure the integrity of their digital photographic records. Images validated by VeriData iDem have been regularly presented in court-rooms since early 2000.

More information can be found at www.signumtech.com.

Spectra Systems Corporation

Spectra Systems works to help businesses mark, sense, track, and authenticate their products from production line to point of purchase.

SysCop™

SysCop is an expansion product offering advanced document security and processing. Spectra also offers a patented digital watermarking technology consisting of the RightMark™ and CaptureMark™ software applications that are designed for protecting printed digital content. These PC-based applications offer many advantages by allowing flexibility in message lengths of the embedded information, and the ability to insert and detect the watermark information by an encrypted security key or PIN. In addition, CaptureMark is being integrated with Spectra's VeriCam™ handheld terminal for instant retrieval of the embedded information from a printed, watermarked image.

More information can be found at www.spsy.com.

Verance

Verance offers innovative audio watermarking solutions to protect, manage, and monitor your audio and visual content, including (1) broadcast monitoring and verification, and (2) copy protection and content management.

ConfirMedia™

ConfirMedia is considered the most comprehensive, reliable system ever created for monitoring television and radio broadcast media. With this system, you can receive next-day verification of broadcast airplay for:

- Television and radio commercials
- Network and syndicated programming
- Program promos
- Music used in commercials and programming

More information can be found at www.verance.com.

WetStone Technologies: Stego Watch

Stego Watch is a forensics service that monitors for stego and analyzes suspected stego images. WetStone's Steganography Detection and Recovery Toolkit is being developed for the Air Force Research Laboratory in Rome, New York. The project overview, according to the company, is "to develop a set of statistical tests capable of detecting secret messages in computer files and electronic transmissions, as well as attempting to identify the underlying steganographic method. An important part of the research is the development of blind steganography detection methods for algorithms."

More information can be found at www.wetstonetech.com.

Chapter 8

Real-World Uses

Medical Records

The use of watermarking in medical records as a method of accurate identification is immediately apparent. With the medical industry migrating more and more toward digital records, watermarking becomes a mandatory addition to prevent mix-ups in patient records. Because of the various protocols and different platforms used in the computer world, data sometimes can become corrupted when it is converted from one format to another. Presently, most image formats separate the image data from the text; an x-ray is separate from the name of the patient, the date of the x-ray, and the name of the physician; if the link between the image and the text were ever broken, things could get bad in a hurry. A way to prevent this is to embed into the image the patient's name and all other pertinent information.

Every patient has an EPR (electronic patient record) made up of examinations, diagnoses, prescriptions, etc., basically a master file containing the record of what has been done with respect to the patient. Using this as an obvious vehicle, a watermarking scheme could be used very effectively.

Watermarking in the medical arena has three main objectives:

1. Hiding metadata, information about the information, to make the image easier to use
2. Integrity control, meaning the image has not been inappropriately modified
3. Authenticity — the image is what the user thinks it is

Two Studies Using Watermarking of Medical Imaging

1. *Authentication and tracing:* Because medical images pass through a number of hands and go through a variety of processes, the introduction of a digital watermark serves as a guarantee that no errors, accidental or otherwise, have been introduced into the image.
2. *EPR diffusion:* If the patient maintains control of his or her own medical record, watermarking is also useful when distributing the record to various sites. Because this record is digital, multiple copies can exist at once; watermarking ensures that the newest is being used and has not been tampered with.

Workplace Communication

In today's workplace where there is a strained balance at best between computer security and employee privacy, steganography could be used as a very effective way of bypassing normal communication channels. Employees should have no expectation of privacy with respect to use of computers in the workplace.

Typically, Hotmail or other Internet-based meeting places are being used as ways of communicating outside and around the firewall. With security and privacy policies at the forefront, steganography may become the next big obstacle security officers have to face when it comes to controlling communication within their networks.

DNA Microdots

Taking what we know about microdots, we will explore the realm of hiding information in a strand of DNA. This provides the sender with a mechanism for hiding a message among a staggeringly large number of similar molecules while keeping the size down to a standard microdot.

A single strand of DNA consists of a chain of simpler molecules called bases, which protrude from a sugar-phosphate backbone. The four varieties of bases are known as adenine (A), thymine (T), guanine (G), and cytosine (C). Any strand of DNA will adhere tightly to its complementary strand, in which T substitutes for A, G for C, and vice versa. For example, a single-stranded DNA segment consisting of the base sequence TAGCCT will stick to a section of another strand made up of the complementary sequence ATCGGA. The links between pairs of bases are responsible for binding together two strands to form the characteristic double helix of a DNA molecule.

Text to DNA Encryption Key

A = CGA	K = AAG	U = CTG	0 = ACT
B = CCA	L = TGC	V = CCT	1 = ACC
C = GTT	M = TCC	W = CCG	2 = TAG
D = TTG	N = TCT	X = CTA	3 = GAC
E = GGC	O = GGA	Y = AAA	4 = GAG
F = GGT	P = GTG	Z = CTT	5 = AGA
G = TTT	Q = AAC	_ = ATA	6 = TTA
H = CGC	R = TCA	, = TCG	7 = ACA
I = ATG	S = ACG	. = GAT	8 = AGG
J = AGT	T = TTC	: = GCT	9 = GCG

They used the encryption key to encode a message reading "JUNE6_INVASION:NORMANDY" as a sequence of 69 bases and synthesized the following DNA strand (Figure 8.1):

AGTCTGTCTGGCTTAATAATGTCTCCTCGAACGATGGGATCTGCTTCT

GGATCATCCCGATCTTTGAAA

Because DNA is a very stable molecule under normal conditions, and PCR is a very sensitive analytic technique, a DNA message can be hidden almost anywhere, Risca notes.

In their proof-of-principle experiment, the researchers dripped a small quantity of DNA-containing solution onto a small dot printed on filter paper. They cut out the dot, taped it over the period in a typed letter, and mailed the letter. The recipient recovered the dot, performed the analysis, and successfully decoded the secret message. Our technique could therefore be used in a similar way to the original microdots: to enclose a secret message in an innocuous letter.

Monitoring of Radio Advertisements

Steganography could be used quite effectively in the automatic monitoring of a radio advertisement or music. An automated system could be set up that watches for a specific stegoed message. This monitoring system could keep track of the number of times an ad is played to ensure the person or company paying for the time is getting full value.

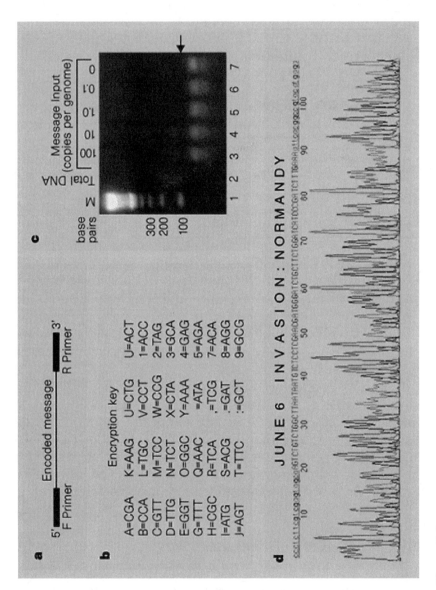

Figure 8.1

Public Key Infrastructure (PKI) and Steganography

A method implementing a public key steganography system has been proposed. Remember the Prisoners' Problem scenario we discussed in Chapter 2? We will assume Alice wants to pass a secret message to Bob, but they did not have the opportunity to exchange a steganographic key before passing the message. If Bob possesses a public key (a PGP key, for example) and Alice knows it, she can encrypt the secret message with Bob's public key, embed the ciphertext in a cover file, and send the resulting stego file to Bob. Bob can extract the ciphertext from the stego file and decrypt it with his private key.

For PKI steganography to work, everyone needs to know how to extract the ciphertext from a stego file. This extraction algorithm can be applied to any cover file and to files without hidden ciphertext. It does not matter if a file actually contains a hidden ciphertext; the result will always be a random-looking bit string, which only a person with the public key will be able to decrypt successfully. To speed up this process in practice, a session key for a symmetric encryption algorithm could be encrypted with the public key and this session key could be used to actually encrypt and decrypt the hidden message.

The drawback is that everyone who receives a stego file will have to extract the potential ciphertext and try to decrypt it with a private key.

Digital Music

Digital watermarks are and will continue to be used to protect music from piracy and to ensure copyrights. As I have discussed in previous chapters, audio watermarking is done by introducing subtle changes into a music file in a particular way. The watermark could be something similar to a particular tone at a particular frequency repeated periodically or something more sophisticated such as simulating the acoustics at the location where the music was recorded, and then altering those acoustics. Some examples of this include BlueSpike's technology that removes a few select tones in a very narrow band. Verance adds signals that are just out of the range of human perception. Others adjust the sound by changing the frequency slightly.

Watermarks in digital music could also carry a variety of information. Some may simply encode a message indicating the file is copyrighted. Another, more sophisticated version could include artist or copyright information (or both). The watermark could even be customized to track down the original owner of a pirated file.

The big enemy of digital watermarks with respect to music is compression. Because compression excludes unwanted information, compression software could be used as a tool for stripping away digital watermarks. Because the watermark typically resides in areas beyond the perceptible auditory range in humans, a compression algorithm would detect and remove it during compression.

The Secure Digital Music Initiative (SDMI), whose charter is to set a common standard for computer, electronic, and entertainment companies, is working with a watermark that simply tries to identify copyrighted music to computers and MP3 players.

Intellectual Property Protection Systems

Digital Rights Management (DRM) Systems

Setup for DRM

To explain the need for Digital Rights Management systems it is best to start out talking about some deficiencies in traditional security models. Technology today and the security models that developed as a result of it primarily grew out of the defense industry. Traditional security models:

1. Are very hierarchical
2. Give governing powers to a system administrator
3. Focus on keeping intruders out

While this works well in a homogenous environment such as a military base, it becomes very cumbersome and impractical when it is thrown into distributed computing environments such as the Internet.

The Resistance to DRM

Another concern that DRM brings with it is that it is a disruptive technology. Two decades ago Hollywood was worried that VCRs would ruin the business of making movies, and prior to that music producers filed lawsuits to prevent radio stations from broadcasting their music to people for free.

As history has shown us, these disruptive technologies have created amazing new market opportunities.

Reasons for DRM: 11 Big Myths about Copyright

1. If it has no copyright notice, it is not copyrighted.
2. If I do not charge for it, it is not a violation.
3. If it is posted to Usenet, it is in the public domain.
4. My posting was just fair use!
5. If you do not defend your copyright, you lose it. Somebody has that name copyrighted!
6. If I make up my own stories, but base them on another work, my new work belongs to me.
7. They cannot get me; defendants in court have powerful rights!
8. Oh, so copyright violation is not a crime or anything?
9. It does not hurt anybody — in fact, it is free advertising.
10. They e-mailed me a copy, so I can post it.
11. So I cannot ever reproduce anything?

Intertrust

Intertrust software and hardware techniques can be implemented in a broad range of products that use DRM and trusted computing technologies, including digital media platforms, Web services, and the enterprise infrastructure.

Madison Project (from IBM)

The Madison Project was the code name for IBM's Electronic Music Management System (EMMS). This system was a stealth initiative to deliver piracy-proof, CD-quality music to consumers via the Internet in the summer of 1999. The AlbumDirect trial began in June and continued through December 1999; the follow-up research extended through mid-January 2000.

EMMS' end-to-end offerings were used to host and distribute music content over the Internet. In addition, EMMS had a clearinghouse capability that protected against unauthorized copying and use of music content by allowing content owners to specify consumer usage parameters and providing transaction reporting for financial clearing. The clearinghouse function is similar in concept to that used by a bank to assure that financial transactions are authorized. Trial participants also used the EMMS client software for music playback.

The experiment was set up at the AlbumDirect.com Web site, and it remains the most comprehensive initiative of its kind to date. The five biggest record companies — BMG Entertainment, EMI Music, Sony Music, Universal Music Group, and Warner Music Group — participated together in the tests. The idea was good except for the fact that MP3s had no copy protection and sites such as Napster sprang up, becoming a serious headache for the record industry.

One of the failings of the Madison Project was that AlbumDirect would not let users pick and choose the tracks they wanted; the purchaser had to buy the whole album. The audio files from Album-Direct were enclosed in a proprietary wrapper allowing the consumer to play the files only on the PC with the company's proprietary player. The AlbumDirect sound files could not be moved directly to a portable MP3 player, and could not be played on a different computer, even if it was networked.

Another drawback was that albums cost $14 or more for just the download, not including the artwork for the album or the blank CD-R. In short, the process was not much less expensive than you would pay for a prepackaged CD of the same album at a retail store or online. For example, AlbumDirect was selling Sarah McLachlan's chart-topping *Fumbling Towards Ecstasy* for $14.38; the same title was available at Amazon.com for $14.99 and at CDnow.com for $15.99. IBM had announced that AlbumDirect would offer 2500 titles, but the actual number in late summer was closer to 1000.

While this may not be the best example for DRM, the potential for a balance between artists' copyrights and royalties weighed against a fair price for the consumer is very apparent, and it is only a matter of time before this technology is used with greater refinement and success.

Cryptolope (IBM)

Another product of IBM is called "cryptolope," which stands for cryptographic envelope. Cryptolope components are all written in Java. In fact, a cryptolope object, the "envelope," is nothing more than a JAR (Java archive) file and is used for secure, protected delivery of digital content. This enables what IBM calls "super distribution"; the package can be moved freely from place to place without losing intactness, authenticity, and associated terms and conditions. Cryptographic envelopes can be compared to secure servers; both approaches use encryption and digital signatures. But cryptographic envelopes go further:

- A single envelope can encompass many different but interrelated types of content — for example, text, images, and audio — and keeps the package intact.
- A cryptolope object is a self-contained and self-protecting object, and can be delivered any way that is convenient. A cryptolope object can be placed on CD-ROMs, FTP sites, or even passed casually from user to user, all without breaking the underlying security.
- A cryptolope object ties the usage conditions of the content to the content itself. One usage condition you frequently set is the price of your cryptolope object, but there are others. You might specify that viewing the content can only be done with a special viewer. Or, for certain types of content, you might specify that it can only be delivered to a system that is capable of applying a digital watermark. Because the cryptolope object is digitally signed, usage conditions cannot be tampered with without invalidating the cryptographic envelope.

A cryptolope system consists of four components:

1. *The builder.* You use this component to build cryptolope objects. It packages the associated files and objects into a cryptolope object, and allows you to set the price and usage conditions you want. You can run the builder in "batch mode," creating cryptolope objects ahead of time, or you can run in "server mode," creating a cryptolope object on demand in response to a particular user's request.
2. *The clearinghouse.* You run this component to unlock your cryptolope objects for your users. Along the way, it verifies the integrity and enforces the terms and usage conditions you set in the cryptolope object.
3. *The opener or cryptolope player.* This component runs on the end user's PC. It protects the user against malicious or anonymous modifications to the cryptolope content. It seamlessly contacts the clearinghouse, unlocks the content to which the user is entitled, and cooperates with the clearinghouse to enforce your wishes.
4. *The lightweight certificate authority.* Digital signatures require digital certificates. The IBM cryptolope system works with standard X.509 certificates. The lightweight certificate authority allows you

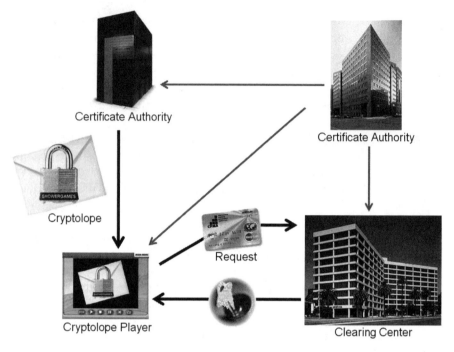

Figure 8.2

to produce your own certificates in cases where these commercially available digital credentials are too expensive or otherwise inappropriate for your application (Figure 8.2).

MagicGate and OpenMG (from Sony)

Sony Corporation is developing a new copyright management technology that could also revolutionize the way in which digital music content is delivered. Two new content protection technologies, tentatively called MagicGate and OpenMG, will provide a solution for protecting digital music on personal computers and personal audio player/recorders that use IC recording media.

MagicGate

MagicGate uses a microchip embedded in both the player and recorder, and media to ensure that protected content is transmitted only between compliant devices and media. All content is transmitted and stored in an encrypted format to prevent unauthorized copying, playback, and transmission of protected content.

MagicGate and OpenMG support the interchange of data between PCs and compliant audio player/recorders, allowing digital music content to be moved rather than copied, while preventing unauthorized copying, playback, and transmission. Sony is planning to broadly license MagicGate and OpenMG to relevant industries. Sony also plans to implement them into Memory Stick and PC-related products.

Super MagicGate

Sony has developed a secure electronic music distribution solution tentatively called Super MagicGate. It includes copyright management, electronic distribution, and content protection technologies for distributing digital music content electronically over the Internet and other digital networks. As with MagicGate and OpenMG, Sony will propose Super MagicGate to the SDMI and actively promote it to the relevant industries.

Super MagicGate features include:

■ *Authentication and content encryption:* Before music content is transmitted, authentication is conducted to ensure that both devices are compliant. If authentication is successfully completed, protected content can then be transferred and recorded in an encrypted format. This provides robust protection against the unauthorized accessing, copying, and distributing of digital music content.

■ *Flexible usage settings:* Super MagicGate accommodates flexible usage settings that give content providers more choice in setting conditions under which digital music content can be provided and enjoyed.

■ *Active rights management:* Usage and billing settings can be changed even after content has been delivered. Users could choose to purchase a music track after sampling it once for free or could receive a limited playback version of a song for upgrade to unlimited playback at a later date.

■ *Offline usage management:* Super MagicGate provides for offline tracking of usage and payment information, which allows flexible content usage and active rights management features to be applied to content enjoyed on portable audio player/recorders and products that are not directly connected to a network.

DRM Summary

■ Almost all things are copyrighted the moment they are written, and no copyright notice is required.

- Copyright is violated whether or not you charged money; damages are determined by what was charged.
- Postings to the Internet are not granted to the public domain and do not grant any permission to do further copying, except perhaps the sort of copying the poster might have expected in the ordinary flow of the Internet.
- Fair use is a complex doctrine meant to allow certain valuable social purposes. Ask yourself why you are republishing what you are posting, and why you could not have just rewritten it in your own words.
- Copyright is not lost because you do not defend it; that is a concept from trademark law. Ownership of names is also from trademark law, so do not think someone has a name copyrighted.
- Fan writings and other work derived from copyrighted works is a copyright violation.
- Copyright law is mostly civil law where the special rights of criminal defendants you hear so much about do not apply. However, new laws are moving copyright violation into the criminal realm.

Systems Built on Encrypted MP3 Files

Mjuice (from Audio Explosion)

Mjuice is a new encrypted file format for audio that uses 128-bit security encryption and is designed to work seamlessly with other software applications. Mjuice has been bought by ArtistDirect, who added this vital piece of technology to its software suite: a secure download solution. ArtistDirect offers digital music downloads in MP3 format, as well as in various secure formats belonging to other companies. Mjuice delivers its catalogue of 30,000 licensed tracks to consumers in a proprietary, secure MP3 format supported by major audio players such as WinAmp and Real Jukebox.

M-Trax (from MCY)

M-Trax technology not only encrypts and watermarks MP3, it also offers its own proprietary digitizing tool, allowing the delivery of CD-quality music. M-Trax philosophy states that focusing on security is a bad idea. M-Trax allows you to play the music at home, at the office, or in the car. It can be taken to a friend's house or, when you have tired of it, sold at a used record store. This solution gives you more flexibility, something you could not do with a normally encrypted MP3 file.

That is exactly what another encrypted-MP3 company, AudioSoft, has accomplished. After three digital copies are made, the copy capacity is disabled.

Key2Audio (from Sony)

Key2AudioXS is a system solution with a sophisticated audio copy control solution, and a clone-proof multimedia part that allows owners of original CDs to enjoy added value in the form of bonus material.

When the disk is inserted into the drive, an authentication process verifies it. If it is the original user, the user gets access to PC playback, CD-Extra content and a Web link. This Web link connects the user directly to a Web area where bonus material of the corresponding disk is available for download or streaming.

Via DRM, Key2AudioXS prevents unauthorized usage, copying, and online distribution. Any further usage is limited and restricted to the PC from which the initial access has been made. Only customers who have purchased the original disk will have access to authorized content.

Super Audio CD (SACD) and DVD-Audio

- New format contains digital watermarks.
- Require special new audio components to work.
- Sony and Philips SACD contains two watermarks: One is for visual verification; the other is invisible and authenticates the disk for playback; without the watermark the disk will not play in a SACD player.
- DVD-Audio disks use technology from Verance, and have acoustic watermarks that cannot be heard by the human ear and must be present for the player to recognize the disk.
- Has not received wide consumer report because of lack of titles, legacy CD, and DVD support.

Recording Industry Association of America (RIAA)

The RIAA is a trade organization that comprises virtually all U.S. record labels and is partnered with dozens of technology firms, including Microsoft and IBM, to develop the Secure Digital Music Initiative (SDMI) to thwart piracy. In total, RIAA is a forum of more than 160 companies and organizations. SDMI specifications were to include MP3 but after a certain time, compliant players would no longer support unprotected MP3 files. While not officially a part of the SDMI, the Madison Project shared the initiative's aim of delivering digitally secure music.

The RIAA is working to develop voluntary, open standards for digital music to enable the widespread Internet distribution of music by adopting a framework that artists and recording and technology companies can use to develop new business models.

The RIAA, along with its sister organizations, IFPI and RIAJ, and the major record companies, was the driving force behind the initial launch of SDMI.

Secure Digital Music Initiative (SDMI)

The SDMI portable device specification is a voluntary, open standard to create and distribute music using unprotected formats, including those who wish to be able to post anonymously. The scope of this is beyond music and includes spoken audio content such as talk shows and audio books.

SDMI-compliant portable players will allow consumers to continue to play music in currently available unprotected digital formats, such as MP3, and also to access music that will only be available through SDMI-compliant digital distribution methods. The SDMI guidelines will offer consumers the opportunity to play and use their music collections in many flexible ways. Portable device specifications will provide for consumers to make personal copies of CDs for playback on their computers and on portable music devices. SDMI will provide artists with the opportunity to reach their fans through new technologies, while respecting and protecting their copyrights.

The MUSE Project (European Union and Recording Industry)

The MUSE project is the European equivalent to the RIAA. Its goal is to create a secure way of distributing music. The MUSE project has four main goals:

- Audibility
- Robustness
- Tamperproof
- Cost

In order to meet these goals, it is clear that audio watermarking technologies will be a vital component of future protection systems for sound recordings. BlueSpike submitted its Giovanni digital watermarking technology to MUSE and is among four proposals being considered out of a total of eight submitted.

There has been little effort thus far to merge audio and video watermarking efforts into a cohesive initiative. While this is not a problem that is being addressed presently, if MUSE chooses two entirely different methods of watermarking, any consumer device designed to handle digital audio and video may have to incorporate two different watermark detectors.

Steganography and the Internet

Since the attacks on the World Trade Center and the Pentagon on September 11th, 2001, there have been a number of articles written about the possibility of Osama bin Laden using steganography to pass messages and coordinate plans. Most of these articles have alluded to the possibility of using steganography, which in reality is ideally suited, but the articles have also provided little tangible proof.

Motivated by these articles, Niels Provos, a doctoral candidate at the University of Michigan working with his advisor, Peter Honeyman, at the Center for Information Technology Integration, developed a steganography detection framework, which he used to analyze two million images from the Internet auction site eBay. The framework consists of three tools:

1. *Crawl:* A Web crawler that downloads images from the Web, used primarily because it is a fast and open source
2. *Stegdetect/Stegbreak:* Tools that identify images that might contain hidden messages, and then guess the secret key required to retrieve a hidden message if it exists
3. *Disconcert:* A distributed computing framework that assists Stegbreak by running it on a cluster of workstations

Following the guidance of an article that mentioned that Amazon and eBay were sites that carried steganographic content, Provos implemented his steganography detection framework and ultimately found nothing.

In October 2001, the American Broadcasting Corporation did a news piece on steganography and produced a stegoed image that was found

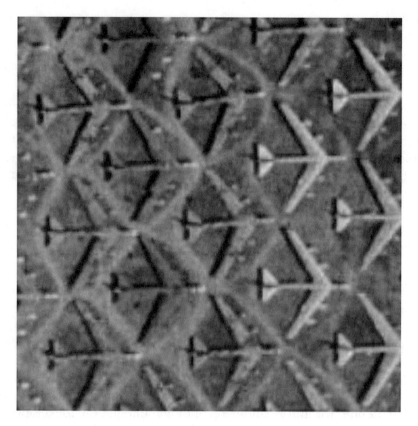

Figure 8.3

"in the wild." The picture was called sovereigntime.jpg, as shown in Figure 8.3. After this, Provos and Honeyman decided to look a little further and began looking at USENET. They analyzed roughly 1 million images, going through an impressive 370,000 a day, and ultimately still found nothing.

Terrorism

After September 11, 2001, the Bush administration responded by requesting that all media outlets use greater discretion when it came to airing statements from Al Qaeda, fearing that the unedited statements might contain secret messages communicated by means of certain words or phrases, combinations of clothing, or discrete nonverbal gestures — in other words: steganography.

In my research I came across one religious extremist site that has set up a page dedicated to using steganography. The title page reads:

Mujahideen, and Islamic Extremist Web site

Mujahideen — Muslim Holy Warriors

The Soldiers of God

Against the Luciferian New World Order — the Dajjal System

And here is an excerpt from the steganography portion of the site:

Encrypted Messages Hidden in Images

Steganography is the art of concealing and sending messages; it has been around as long as people have had secret information to relay. This practice has come a long way since the days of letters with invisible inks carried by midnight messengers or encrypted Morse code delivered over secret radio frequencies. Computers and the World Wide Web provide a new twist on this covert activity. Today's digital cameras produce high-quality images, and the Internet easily and inexpensively carries enormous volumes of information worldwide.

There are hidden messages in the following images; they are invisible to the eye and the images are no different than any other. The messages are encrypted and a password is required to read the messages.

Instructions on how to read the messages and create your own can be found here.

Program to encrypt/decrypt mujahideen.exe (right click, save as) (virus/trojan free, no nasties, we promise)

Actually the mujahideen.exe is really the gifshuffle program, which is described in another section of this book.

The concern at this point is not so much whether terrorists are using steganography for their own devices, but what would reactionary legislation do to the use of steganography by all people? How would this legislation also hinder law enforcement and forensic investigators in charge of detecting this steganography?

Should current stego tools become inaccessible if terrorists are sophisticated enough to use steganography software?

If bin Laden is supposedly using old-fashioned steganography in videotape broadcasts, cracking down on online steganography would do nothing to prevent terrorists or other criminal elements from using more traditional analog means to pass along messages to each other.

While terrorism is certainly one of the more dangerous uses of steganography that face the world today, there are other groups, both good and bad, who could use steganography to keep their communications secret, including:

- Intelligence services
- Corporations with trade secrets to protect
- Organized crime
- Drug traffickers
- Money launderers
- Child pornographers
- Weapons traffickers
- Criminal gangs
- People concerned about government eavesdropping
- People who have to circumvent restrictive crypto laws

Foreign Interest

Germany

According to Bavarian Interior Minister Guenter Beckstein, political extremists are increasingly using modern means of communication, including e-mail, for their propaganda. According to the Office for the Protection of the Constitution, encoding technologies continue to complicate monitoring. In addition to the transmission of encoded data, whose decoding partly requires considerable exertion, steganography is also sporadically used.

Philippines

The University of the Philippines is starting a graduate level course in cryptography and information security. One of the topics included in this course is "Steganography or Message-Hiding."

The Movie Industry

Copy Protection for DVD Video

DVD players were introduced into the consumer market segment in late 1996. The capacity of these disks is significantly larger than audio CDs, 4.7 Gb per side versus 650 Mb. Prerecorded movies use the MPEG-2 compression scheme and are subsequently encrypted prior to being stored on DVD.

Unlike a DVD copy, a copy of a VHS tape looks inferior to the original tape. Thus as second-generation DVD players with digital video recording capabilities continue to be introduced into the marketplace, there is a pressing need to provide several levels of copy protection.

The Supreme Court has held that personal, home videotape recording of a television broadcast for time-shifting purposes is a fair use and therefore does not constitute copyright infringement.

The DVD copy-protection system is designed to support a copy generation management system (CGMS). CGMS/A is used to control the amount of legal copies allowed. The CGMS/A information is embedded in the outgoing video signal. For CGMS/A to work, the equipment making the copy must recognize and respect the CGMS. This requires at least two bits of information to be associated with a piece of video, indicating one of the following copy states:

> "copy_never"
> "copy_once"
> "copy_no_more"
> "copy_freely"

These metadata are problematic in two respects:

1. Getting the metadata out is expensive and the computer industry does not want the responsibility.
2. Copy control could survive analog-to-digital-to-analog conversions, which is where watermarking comes in, and that means that watermarking hardware will need to be in every DVD player.

This leads to the Copy Protection Technical Working Group, which follows two major principles:

1. The copy protection system is not mandatory; devices are either compliant or noncompliant.
2. The system is cost effective.

At present, there are two components that are already being built into consumer devices, the content scrambling system and the analog protection system.

Content Scrambling System (CSS)

- Scrambles MPEG 2.
- Two keys, one to the disk, the other to the MPEG file.
- Keys are stored in the lead area of the disk.
- Usually only works in compliant drives.
- Prevents byte-for-byte copies of a MPEG data stream.
- Encourages the manufacture of compliant drives.

Analog Protection System (APS)

This modifies NTSC/PAL signals so they can be viewed on a TV but not recorded by a VCR. DVDs are not NTSC/PAL encoded, so the encoder must be in the DVD player.

Steganographic File Systems

The steganographic file system is a method of storing files in such a way that encrypts data and hides it so that it cannot be proven to be there. A steganographic file system can:

- Hide users' documents in other seemingly random files.
- Allow the owner to give names and passwords for some files while keeping others secret.
- Behave like a second layer of secrecy. Encrypted files are out in the open and visible but not understandable. Stego files are not even visible and an outsider cannot look for files that "are not there."

A stego file system can protect from some threats:

- Torture to reveal crypto keys or other secrets.
- When conducting delicate negotiations, such as between a company and a trade union, informal offers may be made, which will be denied in the event of later litigation; however, the other side might obtain court orders for access to documents.

The steganographic file system, along with being practical, offers the following functionality:

- Users can plausibly deny certain files being stored on the disk.
- Guaranteed confidentiality of hidden files.
- The deletion of hidden and nonhidden files ensures secure destruction.
- Layers of security can be used, ensuring that the compromise of lower layers does not reveal the presence of higher ones.
- Deniability of the existence of higher layers.
- The installation of the driver can be justified by the additional security advantages it provides.
- Write accesses that are performed while not all hidden layers are open are unlikely to damage data in hidden files.
- Write access to hidden files between inspections cannot be distinguished from nonhidden files that have been created or deleted.
- Nonhidden files are accessible when the StegFS driver and its block allocation table are temporarily removed.
- UNIX file system semantics are implemented.

Bibliography

Anderson, R., Needham, R., and Shamir, A., *The Steganographic File System,* University of Cambridge, U.K.

Bloom, J.A., Cox, I.J., Kalker, T., Linnartz, J.-P.M.G., and Miller, M.L., "Copy Protection for DVD Video," *IEEE,* 87, 7, July 1999.

Boney, L., Twefik, A.H., Hamdy, K.N., *Digital Watermarks for Audio Signals,* Department of Electrical Engineering, 1996.

Borland, J., "Movie Industry Dealt DVD-Cracking Blow," CNET News, November 1, 2001.

Clelland, C.T., Risca, V., and Bancroft, C., "Hiding Messages in DNA Microdots," *Nature,* 399, 533–534, 1999.

Cook, S., "Audio Revolution Blasts Record Companies," *Christian Science Monitor,* April 1999.

Czerwinski, S., Fromm, R., and Hodes, T., *Digital Music Distribution and Audio Watermarking,* Computer Science Division, University of California.

Deutsch, R.W., *More Tales from Encryption,* Wired News, January 1999.

Drummond, M., "The Madison Project: The Future of Downloadable CDs is Here … but Don't Tell Anybody."

Gilbert, B., *Steganography: Why It Matters in a "Post 911" World,* SANS Institute, 2002.

Gong, L., *Digital Watermarking: A Survey and Experiment,* University of Bridgeport, 2002.

Hartung, F. and Girod, B., *Watermarking of Compressed and Uncompressed Video,* University of Erlangen-Nuremberg, 1998.

Herrigel, A., Ruandiadh, J.O., Peterson, H., Pereira, S., and Pun, T., *Secure Copyright Protection Techniques for Digital Images,* University of Geneva.

IBM Cryptolope® Technology, Executive Summary, available at www.ibm.com

Jessup, P., "The Business Case for Audio Watermarking," International Federation of the Phonographic Industry.

Jones, C., "Crypto Creeps into MP3 Domain."

Judge, J.C., *Steganography: Past, Present, and Future,* SANS, 2001.

Katzenbeisser, S. and Petitcolas, F.A.P., (Eds.), *Information Hiding: Techniques for Steganography and Watermarking,* Artech House, Boston, 2000.

Kelley, J., "Terror Groups Hide behind Web Encryption," *USA Today,* February 5, 2001.

Key2Audio, available at www.sony.com

Kirovski, D., Peinado, M., and Petitcolas, F.A.P., *Digital Rights Management for Digital Cinema,* Microsoft Research.

Lacy, J., Quackenbush, S.R., Reibman, A.R., and Snyder, J.H., *Intellectual Property Protection Systems and Digital Watermarking,* AT&T Labs-Research, Florham Park, NJ.

Lau, S., *An Analysis of Terrorist Groups' Potential Use of Electronic Steganography,* SANS Institute, 2002.

MagicGate and OpenMG, available at www.sony.com

McCullagh, D., "Bin Laden: Steganography Master?" Wired News, February 2001.

McDonald, A.D. and Kuhn, M.G., *StegFS: A Steganographic File System for Linux,* University of Cambridge, Computer Laboratory, U.K.

MP3Newswire.net, available at www.mp3newswire.net/sect/archive.htm

Petitcolas, F.A.P., Anderson, R.J., and Kuhn, M.G., "Information Hiding — A Survey," *IEEE,* July 1999.

Provos, N. and Honeyman, P., *Detecting Steganographic Content on the Internet,* Center for Information Technology, University of Michigan, 2001.

Schneier, B. and Wayner, P., "Cryptogram — Terrorists and Steganography," Counterpane Internet Security, Inc., 2001.

Weatherhead, B., "The Digital Link: Understanding the Digital Home Video Controversy on Commercial Content (Copy) Protection," *Home Theater and High Fidelity,* February, 2002.

www.intertrust.com

www.mujahideen.fsnet.co.uk/hidden-messages.htm

Chapter 9

Detection and Attacks

Detection

Statistical Tests

Statistical tests can reveal that an image has been modified by determining that its statistical properties deviate from a norm. Some tests are independent of the data format and measure only the entropy of the redundant data. Expect images with hidden data to have higher entropy.

Stegdetect

Stegdetect is an automated tool for detecting steganographic content in images. It is capable of detecting several different steganographic methods to embed hidden information in JPEG images. Currently, the detectable schemes are (Figure 9.1):

- jsteg
- jphide for UNIX and Windows
- invisible secrets
- outguess 01.3b
- F5 (header analysis)
- appendx and camouflage

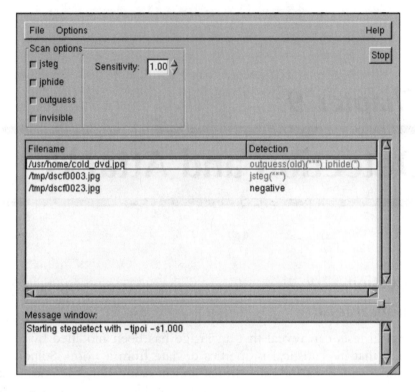

Figure 9.1

An example of the output looks like this:

```
$ stegdetect *.jpg
cold_dvd.jpg : outguess(old)(***) jphide(*)
dscf0001.jpg : negative
dscf0002.jpg : jsteg(***)
dscf0003.jpg : jphide(***)
[...]
$ stegbreak -tj dscf0002.jpg
Loaded 1 files...
dscf0002.jpg : jsteg(wonderland)
Processed 1 file, found 1 embedding.
Time: 36 seconds; Cracks: 324123, 8915 c/s
```

Stegbreak

Stegbreak is a program that uses dictionary guessing to break the encoding password. Stegbreak is used to launch dictionary attacks against jsteg-shell, jphide, and outguess 0.13b.

Dictionary Attacks on Steganographic Systems

A dictionary attack is a brute-force attack that is generally a threat to all passwords. Basically, a dictionary attack works by looking for passwords that are part of a specific list, such as an English dictionary. We will now take a look at how a dictionary attack works on a steganographic system.

Steganographic systems embed header information in front of the hidden message. This header contains information about the length of the message, compression methods, and other important details. A dictionary attack, using the Stegbreak program, will choose a key from the dictionary and use it to try and retrieve the header information. If the header matches, the key has been guessed. The Stegbreak dictionary contains about 1,800,000 words and phrases, including words from the English, German, and French languages; science fiction novels; the Koran; famous movies and songs, etc.

Visible Noise

Attacks and analysis on hidden information may take several forms: detecting, extracting, and disabling or destroying hidden information. Images with too high a payload may display distortions from hidden information. Selecting the proper combination of steganography tools and carriers is important to successful information hiding.

Some images may become quite degraded with even small amounts of embedded information. This "visible noise" will give away the existence of hidden information. The same is true with audio. Echoes and shadow signals reduce the chance of audible noise, but they can be detected with little processing.

Only after evaluating many original images and stego-images with regard to color composition, luminance, and pixel relationships do anomalies point to characteristics that are not "normal" in other images. Patterns become visible when evaluating many images used for applying steganography. Such patterns are unusual sorting of color palettes, relationships between colors in color indexes, and exaggerated "noise."

An approach used to identify such patterns is to compare the original cover-images with the stego-images and note a visible difference, which is the known-cover attack. Minute changes are readily noticeable when comparing the cover- and stego-images. In making these comparisons with numerous images, patterns begin to emerge as possible signatures of steganography software.

Appended Spaces and "Invisible" Characters

This refers back to the technique of hiding data in spaces within text. This form of text semagram uses the white space in a document to denote binary values. The white space can be between the individual words, the sentences, or even between the paragraphs. Almost any combination is possible, but to a point, if the text appears to have too much white space it may be subject to scrutiny. While this form of steganography can work effectively, it has some big drawbacks. First, if the document is digital any modern word processor would be able to show the spacing irregularities or, worse, reformat the document and destroy the hidden information. The other drawback is that this method does not transmit a large amount of information easily, which can limit its practicality.

There are not only spaces between words but also tiny spaces between some letters, either to form a binary code out of the frequency of spaces/no spaces or to indicate that the letter following after the space is part of the secret message. To the naked eye nothing may be apparent, but when put through the scrutiny of a modern word processor the pattern will become very apparent.

Color Palettes

Some tools have characteristics that are unique among stego-tools. In some steganography programs the color palettes have unique characteristics that do not appear anywhere else. For example, the Hide and Seek program creates color palette entries that are divisible by 4 for all bit values. The palette modification creates a detectable steganography signature.

TCP/IP Packet Capture

In TCP/IP, there are a number of methods available whereby covert channels can be established and data can be surreptitiously passed between hosts. This method can be used in a variety of areas:

- Bypassing packet filters, network sniffers, and "dirty word" search engines
- Encapsulating encrypted or nonencrypted information within otherwise normal packets of information for secret transmission through networks that prohibit such activity (TCP/IP steganography)
- Concealing locations of transmitted data by "bouncing" forged packets with encapsulated information off innocuous Internet sites

Protection from this technique would start with the use of an application proxy firewall system. An application proxy firewall is designed to keep packets from logically separated networks from passing directly to each other. A packet-filter firewall is another option, but is not as effective as the application proxy firewall.

Detection of these techniques can be difficult. If the information in the packet data is encrypted or is "bounced" from another server, it can be very difficult to determine where the packet originated. One way to determine where a forged packet originated is to put a sniffer on the inbound side of the server.

Repetitive Patterns (Patchwork)

The patchwork algorithm allows for the detection of a single, specific bit in an image. Patchwork will embed a specific statistic in a host image, a small watermark that tells whether a larger watermark is embedded within an image. In short, patchwork is an indicator that tells a program that the rest of the watermark is present. While this method by itself works quite well, there have been a number of performance improvements made to the patchwork process, including treating patches at several points rather than just one and using visibility masks to avoid putting patches where they would be easily noticed. In some instances, if this technique is used with too much payload, a repetitive pattern may appear in the image.

Attacks

Steganography Attacks

- *Stego-only attack:* Attack is one where we have only the stego-medium, and we want to detect and extract the embedded message (Figure 9.2).

Stego Medium

Figure 9.2

- *Known-cover attack:* Attack is used when we have both the stego-medium and the cover-medium, so that a comparison can be made between the two (Figure 9.3).
- *Known-message attack:* Attack assumes that we know the message and the stego-medium, and we want to find the method used for embedding the message (Figure 9.4).
- *Chosen-stego attack:* Attack is used when we have both the stego-medium and the steganography tool or algorithm (Figure 9.5).

Cover Medium

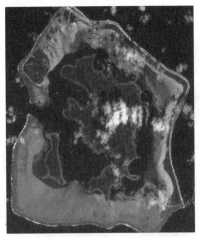

Stego Medium

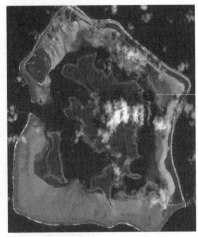

Hash value:
A2F53479JG4FNB621354CD67TG679912

Hash value:
CR341479JG4FNYT462A4CD67TG678UT6

Figure 9.3

- *Chosen-message attack:* Attack is one where the steganalyst generates a stego-medium from a message using a particular tool, looking for signatures that will enable the detection of other stego-media (Figure 9.6).

Disabling or Active Attacks

- *Blur:* Smoothes transitions and decreases contrast by averaging the pixels next to the hard edges of defined lines and areas where there are significant color transitions.
- *Noise:* Random noise inserts random-colored pixels to an image. Uniform noise inserts pixels and colors that closely resemble the original pixels.
- *Noise reduction:* Reduces noise in the image by adjusting the colors and averaging pixel values.
- *Sharpen:* Sharpening is the opposite of blur. It increases contrast between adjacent pixels where there are significant color contrasts, usually at the edge of objects.
- *Rotate:* Rotation moves an image around its center point in a given plane.

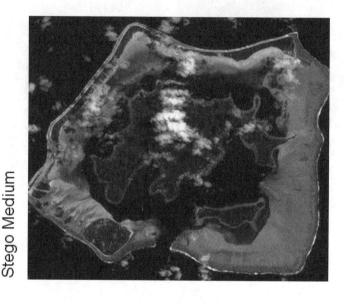

Stego Medium

Message

ADDRESS DELIVERED AT THE DEDICATION

OF THE CEMETERY AT GETTYSBURG

Four score and seven years ago our fathers br
on this continent, a new nation, conceived in L
dedicated to the proposition that all men are cre

Now we are engaged in a great civil war, testi
that nation, or any nation so conceived and so ded
long endure. We are met on a great battle-field c
We have come to dedicate a portion of that field
resting place for those who here gave their live
nation might live. It is altogether fitting and pro
should do this.

But, in a larger sense, we can not dedicate—
consecrate—we can not hallow—this ground. The
living and dead, who struggled here, have consec
above our poor power to add or detract. The wor

Figure 9.4

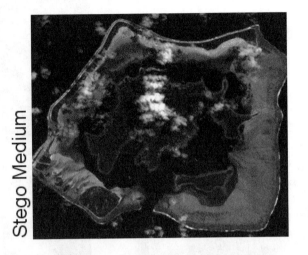

Stego Medium

Steganography Tool
or
Embedding Algorithm

Figure 9.5

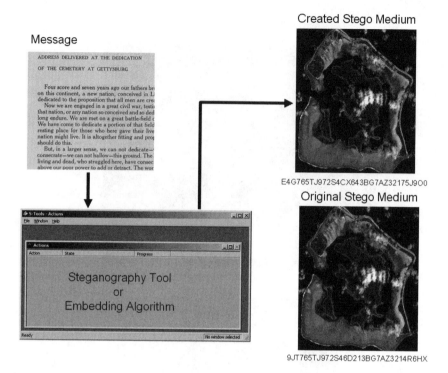

Figure 9.6

- *Resample:* Resampling involves an interpolation process to minimize the "raggedness" normally associated with expanding an image.
- *Soften:* Applies a uniform blur to an image to smooth edges and reduce contrasts, and causes less distortion than blurring.

Watermark Attacks

- *Collusion attack:* By looking at a number of different objects with the same watermark, one can find, isolate, and remove the watermark by comparing the copies.
- *Jitter attack:* The jitter attack works the same in watermarking as it does steganography. Its purpose is to upset the placement of the bits that identify the watermark by applying "jitter" to the image. How robust the watermark is depends on how much jitter it can take; in the case of a fragile watermark, just cropping one row of pixels from the perimeter of the image will change it significantly enough to destroy the watermark. But then again, a fragile watermark is not supposed to be able to endure a jitter attack.

- *StirMark:* The StirMark attack applies small distortions that are designed to simulate the printing or scanning process. If you have ever scanned in a hard-copy photograph, you know that subtle distortions are introduced no matter how careful you are. The placement of the picture on the scanning bed, the conversion process from tangible to digital — all of these shifts can put a watermark to the test. StirMark does all of these automatically and adds multiple distortions on top of one another. Some of the distortions StirMark uses are JPEG, scaling, rotation and cropping, rotation, scale and cropping, shearing, flip, change of aspect ration, row and column removal, and random bending, just to name a few. This attack is particularly effective because some watermarks are more resistant to one type of modification as opposed to another, but usually are not immune to all of them at the same time.

- *Anti soft bot:* A benefit of watermarking in the realm of the Internet is the ability to use software robots, sometimes called soft bots or spiders, to search through Web pages for watermarked images. If the soft bot finds a watermarked image, it can use the information to determine if there is a copyright violation.

- *Attacks on echo hiding:* Echo hiding is a signal-processing technique that places information imperceptivity into an audio data stream in the form of closely spaced echoes. These echoes place digital tags into the sound file with very little sound degradation. Echo hiding is also very resistant to jitter attacks, so a removal attack is the usual method for getting rid of the watermark. In echo hiding, most echo delays are between 0.5 and 3 milliseconds; in anything above 3 milliseconds, the echo becomes noticeable. To remove the echo, the attacker uses the same method as detecting it, only with some modifications. The process of echo detection is called cepstrum analysis and the attacker would use this process with an opposite signal to damage the watermark.

- *Additive noise:* This attack is fairly straightforward; it simply involves adding additional, imperceptible noise to the image to hinder or stop the watermark detection process. Because each pixel in the image has a tolerance for the amount of noise that can be introduced and still remain invisible, the additive noise attack uses that tolerance value to introduce the maximum amount of uncertainty that the decoder will have to deal with.

- *Linear filtering:* Linear filtering is used when an attacker wants to eliminate a watermark or destroy any information that identifies the author or owner. This attack is carried out by removing an estimate of the watermark from the marked image, restoring the original image. Sometimes this "estimate" watermark can cause damage to the data, depending on the complexity of the information the watermark is embedded into.

■ *Resampling:* Resampling combines analysis and interpretation of a data file to change it by a certain factor. What that essentially means is a program will look at an image file, for example, interpret the pixels it "sees," and assign a new approximate value to them. It will also look at the surrounding pixels for more information about the image. Then it takes these new values, based on estimations, and puts everything back together, creating a new image. The tolerances set in the beginning determine how much variance happens during the resampling process.

■ *Cropping:* Often a watermark is embedded in a linear fashion, meaning that the pixels that comprise the watermark follow a pattern that cropping can do significant damage to, depending on the extent of cropping. If the watermark is embedded in a pseudorandom fashion, the watermark may be more resilient to cropping, but removing pixels is still removing pixels, and it will weaken the energy of the watermark.

■ *The mosaic attack:* This attack relies on the fact that a watermark cannot be embedded into a small image. This attack disables the watermark by splitting the image into small pieces and then putting them back together. This creates the illusion that the image is really one picture, not a series of small ones. But as far as the detection method is concerned, it does not see one image; it sees a number of them, and none of them contain the watermark it is looking for.

Bibliography

Anderson, R.J. and Petitcolas, F.A.P., *On the Limits of Steganography.*

Judge, J.C., *Steganography: Past, Present, and Future,* SANS, 2001.

Katzenbeisser, S. and Petitcolas, F.A.P., (Eds.), *Information Hiding: Techniques for Steganography and Watermarking,* Artech House, Boston, 2000.

Stegbreak, available at http://www.citi.umich.edu/u/provos/stego/usenet.php.

Stegdetect, available at http://www.outguess.org/detection.php.

Chapter 10

The Future

This book has chronicled steganography from its beginnings thousands of years ago to its modern uses and methods. With all the variations and possibilities, the question remains: What does the future have in store?

There are some who feel that steganography has many practical uses because it works only when no one expects you to use it. And with steganography getting more and more press these days, it will be something that is looked for all or most of the time.

There are others that feel that steganography will continue to grow in sophistication and ease of use to where reasonable doubt that stego may or may not be used is enough to ensure secrecy.

Some legitimate uses of steganography in the future could be:

- Protection of property, real and intellectual
- Individuals or organizations using steganographic carriers for personal or private information

Some illegal uses of steganography in the future could be:

- Criminal communications
- Fraud
- Hacking
- Electronic payments
- Gambling and pornography

- Harassment
- Intellectual property offenses
- Viruses
- Pedophilia

Steganography in digital form is still a young technology and will only increase in importance in the security community as time goes on. While I do not have a crystal ball for what will take shape in the future, I can offer you some guidelines for being as prepared as possible when changes do happen.

1. Keep yourself informed.
2. If you have to form a defensive strategy, consider the time factor.
3. Apply offensive weaponry in defensive ways.
4. Keep the community informed if you discover a new threat.
5. Do not consider any form of protection you might want to add as too extreme.

Bibliography

Judge, James C., *Steganography: Past, Present, and Future,* SANS, 2001.

Chapter 11

Glossary

ACC: Audio Communications Controller

Acrostic: A poem or series of lines in which certain letters, usually the first in each line, form a name, motto, or message when read in sequence.

Anamorphosis: An image or the production of an image that appears distorted unless it is viewed from a special angle or with a special instrument.

Anonymity: The state in which something is unknown or unacknowledged.

Audio masking: A condition where one sound interferes with the perception of another sound.

Blind scheme: An extraction process method that can recover the hidden message only by means of the encoded data.

Bootleg: An unauthorized recording of a live or broadcast performance, which is duplicated and sold without the permission of the artist, composer, or record company.

Bote-swaine cipher: A steganographic cipher used by Francis Bacon to insert his name within the text of his writings.

Cardano's grille: A method of concealing a message by which a piece of paper has several holes cut in it (the grille), and when it is placed over an innocent-looking message the holes cover all but specific letters, spelling out the message. It was named for its inventor, Girolamo Cardano.

Chosen message attack: A type of attack where the steganalyst generates a stego-medium from a message using some particular tool, looking for signatures that will enable the detection of other stego-media.

Chosen stego attack: A type of attack where both the stego-medium and the steganography tool or algorithm are available.

Cipher disk: An additive cipher device used for encrypting and decrypting messages. The disk consists of two concentric circular scales, usually of letters, and the alphabets can be repositioned with respect to one another at any of the 26 relationships.

Coefficient: A number or symbol multiplied with a variable or an unknown quantity in an algebraic term.

Color palette: A set of available colors a computer or an application can display. Also known as a *CLUT*: **Color Look Up Table.**

Compression: A method of storing data in a format that requires less space than normal.

Counterfeits: Duplicates that are copied and packaged to resemble the original as closely as possible. The original producer's trademarks and logos are reproduced in order to mislead the consumer into believing that he is buying an original product.

Cover escrow: An extraction process method that needs both the original piece of information and the encoded one in order to extract the embedded data.

Cover medium: The medium in which data is hidden; it can be an innocent-looking piece of information for steganography, or an important medium that must be protected for copyright or integrity reasons.

Covert channel: A channel of communication within a computer system or network that is not designed or intended to transfer information.

Cryptolope: Cryptographic envelope, an IBM product. Cryptolope objects are used for secure, protected delivery of digital content by using encryption and digital signatures.

Datagram: A self-contained, independent entity of data carrying sufficient information to be routed from the source to the destination computer without reliance on earlier exchanges between this source and destination computer and the transporting network. The term has been generally replaced by the term *packet*.

Dead drop: A method of secret information exchange where the two parties never meet.

Digimark: A company that creates digital watermarking technology used to authenticate, validate, and communicate information within digital and analog media.

Digital Rights Management (DRM): Focuses on security and encryption to prevent unauthorized copying, limiting distribution to only those who pay. This is considered first-generation DRM; second-generation DRM covers description, identification, trading, protection, monitoring, and tracking of all forms of rights usages over both tangible and intangible assets, including management of rights holders' relationships. It is important to note that DRM manages all rights, not only those involving digital content. Additionally, it is important to note that DRM is the "digital management of rights" and not the "management of digital rights." That is, DRM manages all rights, not only the rights applicable to permissions over digital content.

Discrete cosine transform (DCT): Used in JPEG compression, the discrete cosine transform helps separate the image into parts of differing importance based on the image's visual quality; this allows for large compression ratios. The DCT function transforms data from a spatial domain to a frequency domain.

Distortion: An undesired change in an image or signal; a change in the shape of an image resulting from imperfections in an optical system, such as a lens.

Dithering: Creating the illusion of new colors and shades by varying the pattern of dots in an image. Dithering is also the process of converting an image with a certain bit depth to one with a lower bit depth.

Echo hiding: Relies on limitations in the human auditory system by embedding data in a cover audio signal using changes in delay and relative amplitude. Two types of echos are created, which allows for the encoding of 1s and 0s.

Embedded message: In steganography, it is the hidden message that is to be put into the cover-medium.

Embedding: To cause to be an integral part of a surrounding whole. In steganography and watermarking, refers to the process of inserting the hidden message into the cover-medium.

FDD: Floppy Disk Drive.

Fingerprint: A form of marking that embeds a unique serial number.

File format dependence: A factor in determining the robustness of a piece of stegoed media. Coverting an image from one format to another will usually render the embedded message unrecoverable.

Fourier transform: An image processing tool that is used to decompose an image into its constituent parts or to view a signal in either the time or frequency domain.

Fragile watermark: A watermark that is designed to prove authenticity of an image or other media. A fragile watermark is destroyed, by design, when the cover is manipulated digitially. If the watermark is still intact, then the cover has not been tampered with. Fragile watermark technology could be useful in authenticating evidence or ensuring the accuracy of medical records or other sensitive data.

Frequency domain: The way of representing a signal where the horizontal deflection is the frequency variable and the vertical deflection is the signal's amplitude at that frequency.

Frequency masking: A condition where two tones with relatively close frequencies are played at the same time and the louder tone masks the quieter tone.

Hidden partition: A method of hiding information on a hard drive where the partition is considered unformatted by the host operating system and no drive letter is assigned.

Injection: Using this method, a secret message is put in a host file in such a way that when the file is actually read by a given program, the program ignores the data.

Intellectual property identification: A method of asset protection that identifies or defines a copyright, patent, trade secret, etc., or validates ownership and ensures that intellectual property rights are protected.

Intellectual property management and protection (IPMP): A refinement of digital rights management (DRM) that refers specifically to MPEGs.

Intertrust: A company that develops intellectual property for digital rights management (DRM), digital policy management (DPM), and trusted computing systems.

Invisible ink: A method of steganography using a special ink that is colorless and invisible until treated by a chemical, heat, or special light. It is sometimes referred to as sympathetic ink.

Invisible watermark: An overlaid image that is invisible to the naked eye, but which can be detected algorithmically. There are two different types of invisible watermarks: fragile and robust.

Jargon code: A code that uses words (especially nouns) instead of figures or letter-groups as the equivalent of plain language units.

Jitter attack: A method of testing or defeating the robustness of a watermark. This attack applies "jitter" to a cover by splitting the file into a large number of samples, then deletes or duplicates one of the samples and puts the pieces back together. At this point the location of the embedded bytes cannot be found. This technique is nearly imperceptible when used on audio and video files.

Kerckhoff's Principle: A cryptography principle that states that if the method used to encipher data is known by an opponent, then security must lie in the choice of the key.

Key2Audio: A product of Sony, embedded code that prevents playback on a PC or Mac; prevents track ripping or copying.

Known-cover attack: A type of attack where both the original, unaltered cover and the stego-object are available.

Known-message attack: A type of attack where the hidden message is known to exist by the attacker, and the stego-object is analyzed for patterns that may be beneficial in future attacks. This is a very difficult attack, equal in difficulty to a stego-only attack.

Known-stego attack: An attack where the tool (algorithm) is known and the original cover object and stego-object are available.

Least significant bit steganography: A substitution method of steganography where the right-most bit in a binary notation is replaced with a bit from the embedded message. This method provides "security through obscurity," a technique that can be rendered useless if an attacker knows the technique is being used.

Linguistic steganography: The method of steganography where a secret is embedded in a harmless message (see Jargon code).

Madison Project: A code name for IBM's Electronic Music Management System (EMMS). EMMS is being designed to deliver piracy-proof music to consumers via the Internet.

Magicgate: A memory media stick from Sony designed to allow users access to copyrighted music or data.

Message: In steganography, the data (text, still images, audio, video, or anything that can be represented as a bitstream)a sender wishes to remain confidential.

Microdot: A detailed form of microfilm that has been reduced to an extremely small size for ease of transport and purposes of security.

Mjuice: An online music store that provides secure distribution of MP3s over the Internet. A secure player and a download system allow users to play songs an unlimited number of times, but only on a registered player.

Mosaic attack: A watermarking attack that is particularly useful for images that are distributed over the Internet. It relies on a Web browser's ability to assemble mutiple images so they appear to be one image. A watermarked image can be broken into pieces but displayed as a single image by the browser. Any program trying to detect the watermark will look at each individual piece, and if they are small enough, will not be able to detect the watermark.

M-trax: An encrypted form of MP3 watermarking technology from MCY Music that protects the music industry and artists from copyright infringments.

MUSE Project: An initiative that contributes to the continuing development of intellectual property standards. The MUSE Project focuses on the electronic delivery of media, embedded signaling systems, and encryption technology, with the goal of creating a global standard.

Network propagation system analysis: A way of determining the speed and method of stego-object (or virus) movement throughout a network.

Newspaper code: A hidden communication technique where small holes are poked just above the letters in a newspaper article that will spell out a secret message. A variant of this technique is to use invisible ink in place of holes.

NTSC/PAL: National Television System Committee: The first color TV broadcast system was implemented in the United States in 1953. This was based on the NTSC (National Television System Committee) standard. NTSC is used by many countries on the American continent as well as many Asian countries, including Japan. NTSC runs on 525 lines/frame. PAL (Phase Alternating Line) standard was introduced in the early 1960s and implemented in most countries except for France.European. The PAL standard utilizes a wider channel bandwidth than NTSC, which allows for better picture quality. PAL runs on 625 lines/frame.

Null(s): A meaningless symbol that is included within a message to confuse unintended recipients.

Oblivious scheme: See Blind scheme.

One-time pad: A system that randomly generates a private key, and is used only once to encrypt a message that is then decrypted by the receiver using a matching one-time pad and key. One-time pads have the advantage that there is theoretically no way to "break the code" by analyzing a succession of messages.

Open code: A form of hidden communication that uses an unencrypted message. Jargon code is an example of open code.

OpenMG: A copyright protection technology from Sony that allows recording and playback of digital music data on a personal computer and other supported devices, but prevents unauthorized distribution.

Packet: see Datagram

Patchwork: An encoding algorithm that takes random pairs of pixels and brightens the brighter pixel and dulls the duller pixel and encodes one bit of information in the contrast change. This algorithm creates a unique change, and that change indicates the absence or presence of a signature.

Payload: The amount of information that can be stored in the cover medium. Typically, the greater the payload, the greater the risk of detection.

PCM (Pulse Code Modulation): Is a digital scheme for transmitting analog data.

Perceptual masking: A condition where the perception of one element interferes with the perception of another.

PictureMarc: A DigiMarc application that embeds an imperceptible digital watermark within an image, allowing copyright communication, author recognition, and electronic commerce. It is currently bundled with Adobe Photoshop.

Piracy (or simple piracy): The unauthorized duplication of an original recording for commercial gain without the consent of the rightful owner; the packaging of pirate copies that is different from the original.

Pirate copies are often compilations, such as the "greatest hits" of a specific artist, or a genre collection, such as dance tracks.

Pixel: Short for Picture Element, a pixel is a single point in a graphic image. It is the smallest thing that can be drawn on a computer screen. All computer graphics are made up of a grid of pixels. When these pixels are painted onto the screen, they form an image.

Raster image: An image that is composed of small points of color data called pixels. Raster images allow the representation of complex shapes and colors in a relatively small file format. Photographs are represented using raster images.

RGB (Red, Green, Blue): Refers to a system for representing the colors to be used on a computer display.

Recording Industry Association of America (RIAA): A trade group that represents the recording industry in the United States. The RIAA works to create a business and legal environment that supports the record industry and seeks to protect intellectual property rights.

Robust watermark: A watermark that is very resistant to destruction under any image manipulation. This is useful in verifying ownership of an image suspected of misappropriation. Digital detection of the watermark indicates the source of the image.

Secure Digital Music Initiative (SDMI): A forum of more than 160 companies and organizations representing a broad spectrum of information technology and consumer electronics businesses, Internet service providers, security technology companies, and members of the worldwide recording industry working to develop voluntary, open standards for digital music. SDMI is helping to enable the widespread Internet distribution of music by adopting a framework that artists and recording and technology companies can use to develop new business models.

Semagram: Semantic symbol. Semagrams are associated with a concept and do not use writing to hide a message.

Slack space: The unused space in a group of disk sectors; the difference in empty bytes of the space that is allocated in clusters minus the actual size of the data files.

Spatial domain: The image plane itself; the collection of pixels that composes an image.

Spread-spectrum image steganography: A method of steganographic communication that uses digital imagery as the cover signal.

Spread-spectrum techniques: The method of hiding a small or narrowband signal (message) in a large or wideband cover.

Steganalysis: The art of detecting and neutralizing steganographic messages.

Steganalyst: One who applies steganalysis with the intent of discovering hidden information.

Steganographic file system: A method of storing files in a way that encrypts data and hides it such that it cannot be proven to exist.

Steganography: The method(s) of concealing the existence of a message or data within seemingly innocent covers.

Stego-only attack: An attack where only the stego-object is available for analysis.

Stegokey: A key that allows extraction of the secret information out of the cover.

Stego-medium: The resulting combination of a cover-medium and embedded message and a stego key.

StirMark: A method of testing the robustness of a watermark. StirMark is based on the premise that many watermarks can survive a simple manipulation to the file, but not a combination of manipulations. It simulates a process similar to what would happen if an image was printed and then scanned back into the computer by stretching, shearing, shifting, and rotating an image by a tiny random amount.

Substitution: The steganographic method of encoding information by replacing insignificant bits from the cover with the bits from the embedded message.

Supraliminal channel: A feature of an image that is impossible to remove without gross modifications, i.e., a visible watermark.

Technical steganography: The method of steganography where a tool, device, or method is used to conceal a message, e.g., invisible inks and microdots.

Temporal masking: A form of masking that occurs when a weak signal is played immediately after a strong signal.

Texture block coding: A method of watermarking that hides data within the continuous random texture patterns of an image. The technique is implemented by copying a region from a random texture pattern found in a picture to an area that has similar texture, resulting in a pair of identically textured regions in the picture.

The Prisoners' Problem: A model for steganographic communication.

Time domain: The way of representing a signal where the vertical deflection is the signal's amplitude, and the horizontal deflection is the time variable.

Traffic security: A collection of techniques for concealing information about a message to include existence, sender, receivers, and duration. Methods of traffic security include call-sign changes, dummy messages, and radio silence.

Transformation analysis: The process of detecting areas of image and sound files that is unlikely to be affected by common transformations and hide information in those places. The goal is to produce a more robust watermark.

Transform domain techniques: Various methods of signal and image processing (Fast Fourier Transform, Discrete Cosine Transform, etc.) used mainly for the purpose of compression.

Vector image: A digital image that is created through a sequence of commands or mathematical statements that places lines and shapes in a given two- or three-dimensional space.

Visible watermark: A visible and translucent image that is overlaid on a primary image. Visible watermarks allow the primary image to be viewed, but still marks it clearly as property of the owner. A digitally watermarked document, image, or video clip can be thought of as digitally "stamped."

Visible noise: The degradation of a cover as a result of embedding information. Visible noise will indicate the existence of hidden information.

Watermarking: A form of marking that embeds copyright information about the artist or owner.

Wrapper: See Cover-medium.

XOR: The XOR (exclusive-OR) gate acts in the same way as the logical "either/or." The output is "true" if either, but not both, of the inputs are "true." The output is "false" if both inputs are "false" or if both inputs are "true." Another way of looking at this circuit is to observe that the output is 1 if the inputs are different, but 0 if the inputs are the same.

YCbCr: A setting used in the representation of digital images. Y is the luminance component; Cb,Cr are the chrominance components.

Index

Note: Italicized pages refer to illustrations